Venice

COLLINS
Glasgow & London

First published 1990
Copyright © William Collins Sons & Company Limited
Published by William Collins Sons & Company Limited
Printed in Hong Kong
ISBN 0 00 435787-6

HOW TO USE THIS BOOK

Your Collins Traveller Guide will help you find your way around your chosen destination quickly and easily. It is colour-coded for easy reference:

The blue-coded 'topic' section answers the question 'I would like to see or do something; where do I go and what do I see when I get there?' A simple, clear layout provides an alphabetical list of activities and events, offers you a selection of each, tells you how to get there, what it will cost, when it is open and what to expect. Each topic in the list has its own simplified map, showing the position of each item and the nearest landmark or transport access, for instant orientation. Whether your interest is Architecture or Sport you can find all the information you need quickly and simply. Where major resorts within an area require in-depth treatment, they follow the main topics section in alphabetical order.

The red-coded section is a lively and informative gazetteer. In one alphabetical list you can find essential facts about the main places and cultural items - 'What is La Bastille?', 'Who was Michelangelo?' - as well as practical and invaluable travel information. It covers everything you need to know to help you enjoy yourself and get the most out of your time away, from Accommodation through Babysitters, Car Hire, Food, Health, Money, Newspapers, Taxis and Telephones to Zoos.

Cross-references: Type in small capitals - **CHURCHES** - tells you that more information on an item is available within the topic on churches. A-Z in bold - **A-Z** - tells you that more information is available on an item within the gazetteer. Simply look under the appropriate heading. A name in bold - **Holy Cathedral** - also tells you that more information on an item is available in the gazetteer under that particular heading.

Packed full of information and easy to use - you'll always know where you are with your Collins Traveller Guide!

*Photographs by **Michael Dent** & **Keith Allardyce***

INTRODUCTION

For more than 500 years writers and travellers have marvelled at
Venice, and sung the praises of that 'city of wonders' in prose and
verse. The poet Shelley thought that the city's buildings were 'like fabrics of enchantment piled to heaven', and to Lawrence Durrell, Venice
gave the impression that 'some great master had burst his whole colour-
box against the sky'.

If ever a city has been a byword for beauty and grace, love and volup-
tuous pleasure, that city is Venice. How apt, then, that Venice seems to
have risen from the waters in the same way as Venus,
goddess of love, is supposed to have done. To
approach the city from the sea is to feel that the event
is new, that the city is emerging before one's eyes,
domes and pinnacles and towers slowly materializing
on a hazy horizon. And indeed, the idea is not so fan-
ciful, as there is a sense in which Venice really has
risen from the waters. Those ornate and elaborate
buildings have grown not from stone foundations sunk
into firm earth but from millions of wood piles sunk
into the soft mud of a lagoon. The stones of Venice,
with their hues of delicate pink and faded ochre,
touched here and there with gold and azure, stand on
what was once a forest of larch and oak.

Founded in the 5thC by refugees escaping from barbar-
ian invasions on the mainland, Venice became a powerful independent republic and prospered from its
favourable position for trade between Europe and the
East. In the late 13thC the Venetian, Marco Polo, trav-
elled the silk road to China and, in his memoirs, gave
us one of the earliest European descriptions of the Far
East. The memoirs were written in a Genoese prison,
after Polo had been taken prisoner in the wars between
Venice and Genoa. Venice eventually defeated her
great rival, Genoa, in 1380, and by then she was a
great maritime and commercial power, extending her
rule and influence over the eastern Mediterran-ean, the
Aegean and beyond. 'Once did she hold the gorgeous

East in fee, and was the safeguard of the West', wrote Wordsworth in his famous poem on Venice. Many castles and fortresses, their walls adorned with the Venetian Lion of St Mark, still stand today in Greece and elsewhere as testimony to Venice's once-great past. Gradually, however, with the discovery of new trading routes and the rise of new empires, the city's power declined. Napoleon overthrew the Venetian Republic in 1797, and in 1866 Venice became part of the new kingdom of Italy.

Piazza San Marco

The Venetian lagoon, sickle-shaped and 544 square kilometres in area, forms the north-western corner of the Adriatic, where Italy curves towards Yugoslavia. South east of the city, on a long island dividing the lagoon from the open sea, is the Lido, a popular seaside resort. Venice itself stands on an archipelago of 117 small, low-lying islands in the centre of the lagoon, and is connected to the mainland by a road and rail viaduct.

As first wooden and later stone buildings rose on the archipelago, so the natural waterways became formalized into canals. Venice today is reputed to have 177 canals, crossed by 450 bridges. 'STREETS FULL OF WATER. PLEASE ADVISE', read the telegram despatched from Venice by the American humorist Robert Benchley. But in fact the city has several kinds of 'street', not just canals. There are many delightful alleyways and passages criss-crossing the city, and these are blessedly free of any motorized traffic. For transport, you must take to the canals. The Grand Canal, the great highway of Venice which bisects the city, offers the full range of options: you can glide along it - at no more than 9 kph - on a gondola, gondola ferry, water-bus, motor launch, or motorized water-taxi.

The Grand Canal is a breathtaking spectacle. Over three kilometers in length and ample in width, it is lined on each side by a virtually unbroken line of palaces, some 200 in all, dating mostly from the 14th to the 18thC. Most of these palaces stand flush to the water, and all are made doubly beautiful by their shimmering reflections.

Venice has so many gems of architecture - an extraordinary 96 per cent of the buildings are listed as historical monuments. Every visitor, of course, goes to the famous St Mark's Square, the Piazza San Marco, the immense arcaded square that is the heart of the city. There can be seen the magnificent Basilica di San Marco, the Campanile, and the astonishing Doge's Palace. But for visitors with time to explore, St Mark's Square is only the beginning of the treasure-house. Throughout the city there are palaces and churches, great and small, jewels of Byzantine, Gothic and Renaissance architecture. And if that were not enough, the city also houses the world's finest collection of Venetian paintings, with works by Bellini, Titian, Tintoretto, Veronese, Canaletto, Tiepolo … The names read like a history of Western Art, and it is tempt-

ing to try to take in too much of this rich feast. Better to concentrate on a few paintings or painters, and then to wander down some quiet alley-ways, absorbing the magic of the city.

For what is most ravishing about Venice lies not in the particular, but in the whole. The city is a work of art in itself, the supreme achievement of the Republic whose fortunes the city mirrored. But Venice is also being ravished; time and the relentless surge of the sea eat away at the foundations of the city. High tides, pollution from nearby Mestre, the wash from motor boats along the canals, and the tread of countless feet are wearing away the city's fabric. The Italian government and the Venice in Peril Fund* work to restore and preserve the buildings and their priceless art treasures, though these efforts are not helped by the gradual sinking of the floor of the lagoon and the consequent rise in the sea-level. But for today, visitors can still marvel at this magical place, this 'paradise of cities'. Long may Venice hold her head above the waters of the lagoon!

*For information, write to the Venice in Peril Fund, 24 Rutland Gate, London SW7 1BB.

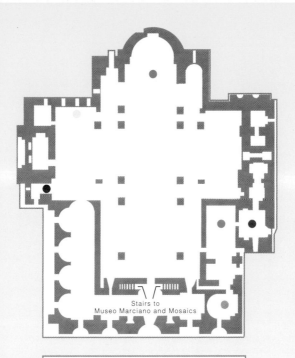

Stairs to
Museo Marciano and Mosaics

● CAPPELLA DELLA MADONNA DI MASCOLI
○ CAPPELLA DELLA MADONNA DI NICOPEIA
● PRESBITERIO
● BATTISTERO
● TESORO
● CAPPELLA ZEN

CAPPELLA DELLA MADONNA DI MASCOLI
A 15thC chapel used by a confraternity of laymen, the Mascoli *('Males' in Venetian dialect). The statues are by Bartolomeo Bon and date from 1430.*

CAPPELLA DELLA MADONNA DI NICOPEIA
The icon in this chapel was stolen by the Venetians from the Byzantine army who carried it into battle as a talisman. It dates from the 12thC.

PRESBITERIO
•L. 1000.
*Separated from the nave by a magnificent marble rood screen bearing statues of the Virgin, St Mark and the Apostles, the Presbytery contains the Pala d'Oro (see **A-Z**) and, beneath the altar, the sarcophagus of St Mark.*

BATTISTERO
*The Baptistery features more mosaics, the 14thC tombs of two doges and a beautiful font (1545) by Sansovino (see **A-Z**), who is also buried here.*

TESORO
•0830-1700 Mon.-Sat, 1400-1630 Sun. (summer); 1000-1630 Mon.-Sat., 1400-1630 Sun. (winter).•L. 2000.
A dazzling treasure collection, most of it looted from Byzantium when the Venetians and the Crusaders captured the city in 1204.

CAPPELLA ZEN Entrance via Battistero.
Named after Cardinal Giambattista Zen who bequeathed his fortune to the Republic on condition that he be buried in the Basilica.

MOSAICS
Climb up to the galleries for a closer look at some of the most precious mosaics in the world - over 4000 m^2 dating from 11th-19thC.

MUSEO MARCIANO First floor.
•0930-1700 (summer), 1000-1630 (winter).•L. 2000.
Fragments of mosaics, superb tapestries, Persian carpets and the original bronze horses of St Mark.

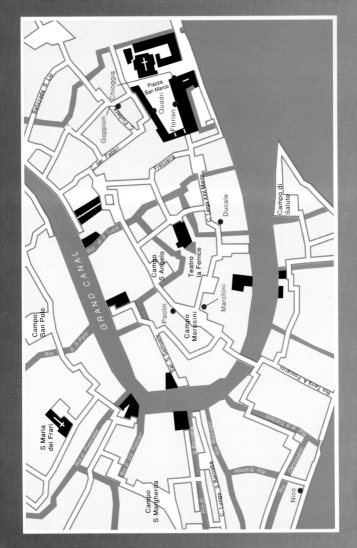

FLORIAN Piazza S Marco 56-59, S Marco.
•0900-2330 Thurs.-Tues. Line 1, 2, 4, S Marco. •Expensive.
The lavish decor is mid 19thC, although the cafe was opened by Floriano
Francesconi in 1720. Only the prices are ahead of their time.

QUADRI Piazza S Marco 11, S Marco.
•0930-2300 (Tues.-Sun. in winter). Line 1, 2, 4, S Marco. •Expensive.
Renowned rival to Florian's, with a pleasant sunny terrace.

CHIOGGIA Piazzetta S Marco 11, S Marco.
•0900-2330 Wed.-Mon. Line 1, 2, 4, S Marco. •Expensive.
Live music and a terrace facing the Gothic splendour of the Doges' Palace.

DUCALE Calle delle Ostreghe, S Marco 2354.
•0745-2130 (2030 in winter) Fri.-Wed. Line 1, S M. del Giglio.
•Moderate.
Delicious sandwiches and exotic cocktails at reasonable prices.

PAOLIN Campo Francesco Morosini, S Marco 2962.
•0800-2400 (2200 in winter) Sat.-Thurs. Line 1, 2, 4, Accademia.
•Moderate.
Situated on a spacious campo and renowned for its fabulous ice-cream.

NICO Zattere, Dorsoduro 922.
•0700-2300 (2100 in winter) Fri.-Wed. Line 5, 8, Zattere.
•Moderate.
Located on the sunny quays on Dorsoduro's southern side, this is the perfect
place for a morning break for cappuccino and toasted sandwiches.

GOPPION Merceria dell'Orologio, S Marco 220.
•0700-2000 Mon.-Sat. Line 1, 2, 4, S Marco. •Moderate.
At the heart of the S Marco shopping area. Serves the best coffee in Venice.

MARCHINI Calle del Spezier, S Marco 2769.
•0800-2030 Wed.-Mon. Line 1, 2, 4, Accademia. •Moderate.
The city's finest pastry shop. Eat in or take away.

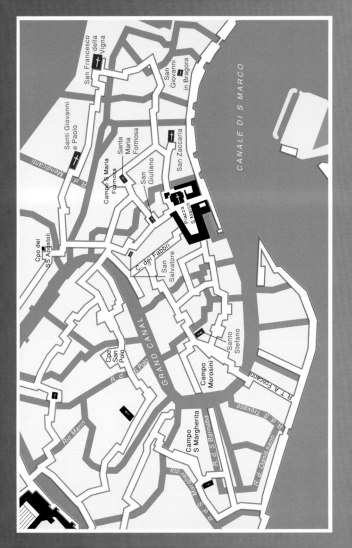

Central & East

SANTI GIOVANNI E PAOLO Cpo SS Giovanni e Paolo, Castello.
●0700-1230, 1530-1930. Line 5, Ospedale Civile; 1, 4, Rialto.
A massive red-brick Gothic structure which took almost a century to build. It houses the tombs of 25 doges as well as superb works of art. See **A-Z**.

SAN ZACCARIA Campo S Zaccaria, Castello.
●0900-1200, 1600-1800. Line 1, 2, 4, S Zaccaria.
A striking blend of Gothic and Renaissance styles. See **WALK 2**, **A-Z**.

SAN SALVATORE Merceria S Salvador, S Marco.
●0900-1200, 1600-1900. Line 1, 4, Rialto.
The Baroque facade of this early-16thC church contrasts sharply with the Renaissance style of its basic structure. See **A-Z**.

SAN FRANCESCO DELLA VIGNA Cpo d. Confraternita, Castello.
Line 5, Celestia.
Built by Sansovino (see **A-Z***) in the 16thC for the Franciscans, on the site of a former vineyard. The facade is by Palladio (see* **A-Z***). See* **WALK 2**.

SANTA MARIA FORMOSA Campo S Maria Formosa, Castello.
●0830-1230, 1730-1900. Line 1, 4, Rialto; 1, 2, 4, S Zaccaria.
One of Codussi's (see **A-Z***) finest churches, with an impressive Baroque campanile which sports a bizarre carved mask at its base. See* **A-Z**.

SANTO STEFANO Campo Francesco Morosini, S Marco.
●0830-1130, 1600-1900. Line 1, 2, 4, Accademia.
A superb Gothic church with a beautiful ship's-keel ceiling. See **A-Z**.

SAN GIULIANO Campo S Zulian, S Marco.
Line 1, 2, 4, S Marco; 1, 4, Rialto.
This mid-16thC church houses works by Palma il Giovane and Veronese.

SAN GIOVANNI IN BRAGORA Cpo Bandiera e Moro, Castello.
●0830-1100, 1700-1900. Line 1 Arsenale; 1, 2, 4, S Zaccaria.
An attractive church, on a delightful campo*, containing works by Palma il Giovane and Cima da Conegliano. Vivaldi was baptized here. See* **WALK 2**.

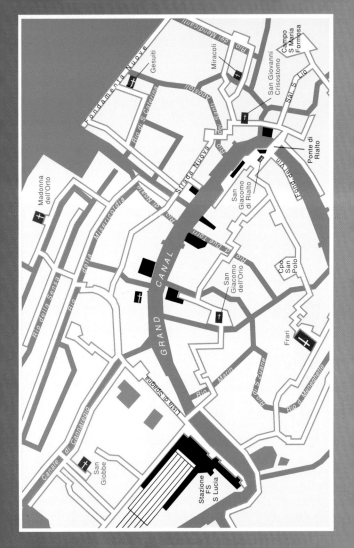

Central & North

FRARI Campo dei Frari, S Polo.
●0900-1200, 1430-1830 Mon.-Fri., 1500-1830 Sun. (Easter-30 Sept.);
0930-1200, 1500-1730 (1 Oct.-Easter). Line 1, 4, S Tomà. ●L. 800.
A magnificent Gothic church with an austere, typically Franciscan, interior housing some of Titian's major works. See **A-Z**.

MADONNA DELL'ORTO Campo dell'Orto, Cannaregio.
●0930-1200, 1530-1700. Line 5, Madonna dell'Orto.
One of the most charming Gothic churches in Venice. See **WALK 3**, **A-Z**.

GESUITI Campo dei Gesuiti, Cannaregio.
Line 5, Fondamenta Nuove.
An 18thC Baroque church with a lavish interior. See **WALK 3**, **A-Z**.

MIRACOLI Campo dei Miracoli, Cannaregio.
●0900-1200, 1500-1800 Mon.-Sat. (Easter-30 Sept.); 0900-1200, 1500-1600 Mon.-Sat. (1 Oct.-Easter). Line 1, 4, Rialto.
An exquisite marble-clad church designed by P. Lombardo. See **A-Z**.

SAN GIACOMO DI RIALTO Campo S Giacomo, S Polo.
Line 1, 4, Rialto.
Founded c.421, making it the oldest church in the city.

SAN GIOBBE Campo S Giobbe, Cannaregio.
Line 5, Ponte Tre Archi; 1, 4, 5, Ferrovia.
A 15thC Tuscan-Renaissance building with sculptures by P. Lombardo.

SAN GIOVANNI CRISOSTOMO Campo S G. Crisostomo,
Cannaregio.
●0800-1230, 1530-1930. Line 1, 4, Rialto.
Codussi's (see **A-Z***) last work contains masterpieces by Giovanni Bellini and Sebastiano del Piombo.*

SAN GIACOMO DELL'ORIO Campo S G. dell'Orio, S Croce.
●0800-1200, 1630-2000. Line 1, S Stae, Riva di Biasio.
An ancient church housing paintings by Veronese, P. il Giovane and Lotto.

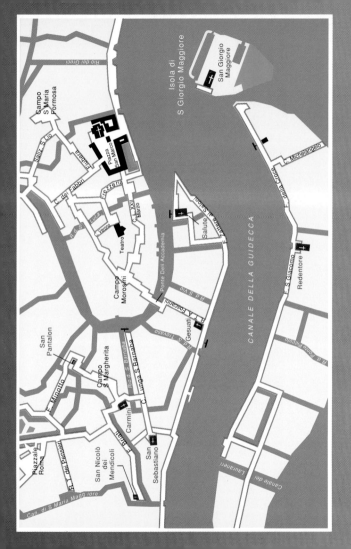

South

SALUTE Campo della Salute, Dorsoduro.
●0900-1200, 1500-1800. Line 1, Salute.
The largest Baroque church in Venice, erected after the great plague of 1630. See **WALK 1, A-Z**.

SAN GIORGIO MAGGIORE Isola di S Giorgio.
●0900-1230, 1400-2030. Line 5, 8, S Giorgio.
This Renaissance church constitutes one of the highlights of the lagoon. See **A-Z**.

REDENTORE Campo Redentore, Giudecca.
●0700-1200, 1530-1930. Line 5, 8, Redentore.
A simple yet majestic building (begun in 1576) by Palladio. See **A-Z, Events**.

SAN SEBASTIANO Campo San Sebastiano, Dorsoduro.
●1000-1300, 1400-1900. Line 5, 8, S Basilio.
A once-modest church which was enriched by some of Veronese's most outstanding works. The artist himself is buried here. See **A-Z, Veronese**.

GESUATI Fondamenta delle Zattere, Dorsoduro.
Line 5, 8, Zattere.
A large Rococo church with frescoes by G. B. Tiepolo. See **WALK 1, A-Z**.

CARMINI Campo Carmini, Dorsoduro.
Line 1, Ca' Rezzonico; 5, 8, S Basilio.
A 14thC church containing some intriguing works of art. See **A-Z**.

SAN PANTALON Campo S Pantalon, Dorsoduro.
●0800-1130, 1630-1900. Line 1, 4, S Tomà.
Baroque church with a remarkable ceiling canvas painted by G. A. Fumiani, who fell from the scaffolding while executing it and was buried here.

SAN NICOLÒ DEI MENDICOLI Campo S Nicolò, Dorsoduro.
●0900-1200, 1600-1900. Line 5, 8, S Basilio.
One of the city's oldest churches. A mixture of styles gives it an unforgettable charm. Inside are some unusual 15th-16thC wood sculptures.

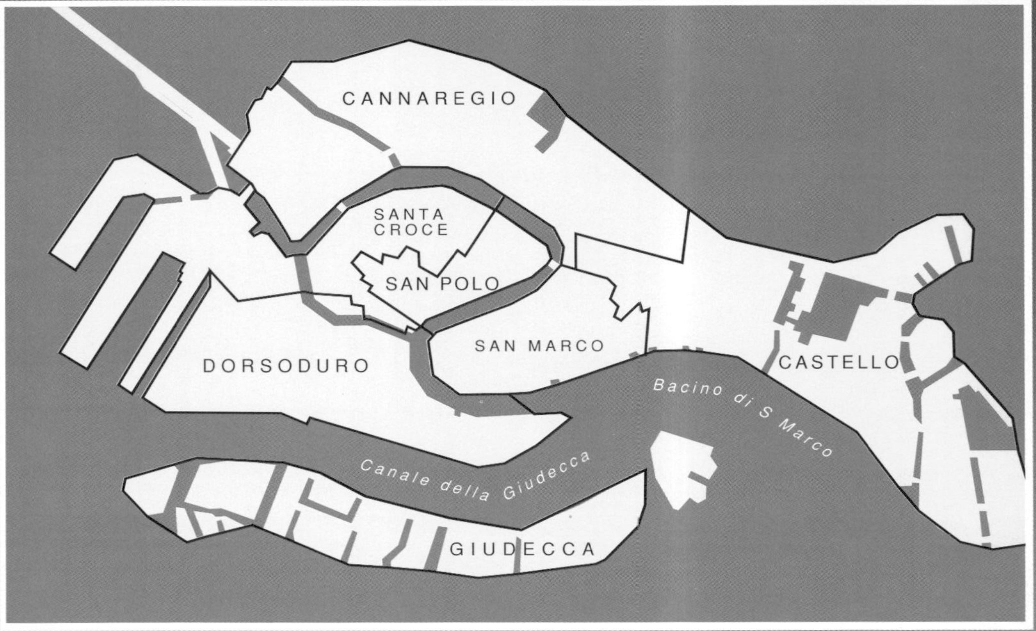
CANNAREGIO
SANTA CROCE
SAN POLO
SAN MARCO
CASTELLO
DORSODURO
Bacino di S Marco
Canale della Giudecca
GIUDECCA

SAN MARCO Line 1, 2, 4, S Marco.
The historical heart of the city as well as its thronging commercial centre. Pigeons and palaces, churches and cafés, mosaics and markets and, of course, tourists.

CASTELLO Line 1, 2, 4, S Zaccaria; 1 Arsenale, Giardini.
The largest of the six sestieri *(see **A-Z**) of Venice, Castello offers many contrasts - from the broad quays of the Riva degli Schiavoni to the narrow* calle *of the island of S Pietro, from the calm of the Giardini Pubblici to the splendour of SS Giovanni e Paolo (see **A-Z**).*

SAN POLO Line 1, S Tomà, S Silvestro.
The smallest of the city's districts has a charm all of its own. Many Venetians congregate on its quiet campi, *thereby avoiding the tourists who outnumber them in S Marco.*

SANTA CROCE Line 1, 4, 5, Ferrovia; 1, Riva di Biasio.
It's worth venturing off the beaten track in this charming part of the city to explore its labyrinthine streets, picturesque canals and deserted campi.

CANNAREGIO Line 1, San Marcuola; 5, Madonna dell'Orto.
*The church of Madonna dell'Orto (see **CHURCHES 2**) entices many to this peaceful district in the north of the city, stretching from the station to the church of the Gesuiti. At its heart lies what was the first ever Ghetto (see **A-Z**). See **WALK 3**.*

DORSODURO Line 1, 2, 4, Accademia; 1, Ca' Rezzonico; 5, Zattere.
An area containing numerous well-restored palazzi, *traditional canal houses, fine buildings such as the Ca' Rezzonico (see **A-Z**) and the Salute (see **A-Z**), and the sunny quays of the Zattere (see **A-Z**). See **WALK 1**.*

GIUDECCA Line 5, 8, Zitelle, Redentore, S Eufemia.
*This district, almost a suburb of the city, was much favoured by wealthy Venetians in the days of the Republic. Its most notable sights range from the indisputably magnificent Redentore (see **CHURCHES 3**, **A-Z**) to the bizarre Mulino Stucky, a massive (derelict) flour mill.*

SECOND FLOOR

FIRST FLOOR

GROUND FLOOR

- ● PORTA DELLA CARTA
- ● SCALA DEI GIGANTI
- ● SALA DEL MAGGIOR CONSIGLIO
- ● SCALA D'ORO
- ● SALA DEL SENATO
- ● SALA DEL COLLEGIO
- ● SALA DEL CONSIGLIO DEI DIECI
- ● SALA DELLA BUSSOLA
- ● SALA D'ARMI DEL CONSIGLIO DEI DIECI

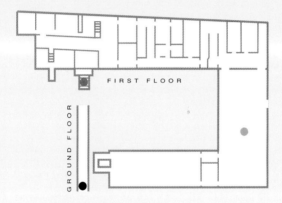

PORTA DELLA CARTA
The name (Door of Paper) may either derive from the fact that decrees were posted here, or from the fact that the state archives were nearby. It was built in the 15thC for Doge Foscari, whose carved image is above the door.

SCALA DEI GIGANTI
A magnificent 15thC staircase. The name refers to Sansovino's (see A-Z) giant statues of Neptune and Mars standing at the top.

SALA DEL MAGGIOR CONSIGLIO First Floor.
The largest and most sumptuous room, and the meeting place of the Great Council. Note Tintoretto's Paradise, the largest oil painting in the world.

SCALA D'ORO
Sansovino also designed this superb staircase (c.1555), which is lavishly decorated with gold stucco work, gaining it the name 'Staircase of Gold'.

SALA DEL SENATO Second Floor.
The Senate's 120 members met here to legislate on the day-to-day affairs of the Republic. Works by Tintoretto adorn the walls and ceiling.

SALA DEL COLLEGIO Second floor.
Here the doge assembled his collegio, or cabinet, who oversaw all state affairs and legislation. The room features superb frescoes by Veronese.

SALA DEL CONSIGLIO DEI DIECI Second Floor.
The meeting place of the Council of Ten (see Doge). The walls are decorated with frescoes by Veronese.

SALA DELLA BUSSOLA Second Floor.
A waiting room for those appearing before the Council of Ten. Note the Bocca di leone (Lion's Mouth) where secret denunciations were placed.

SALA D'ARMI DEL CONSIGLIO DEI DIECI Second Floor.
One of the finest armouries in Europe. Make sure you see the magnificent suit of white armour presented to the city by King Henry IV of France.

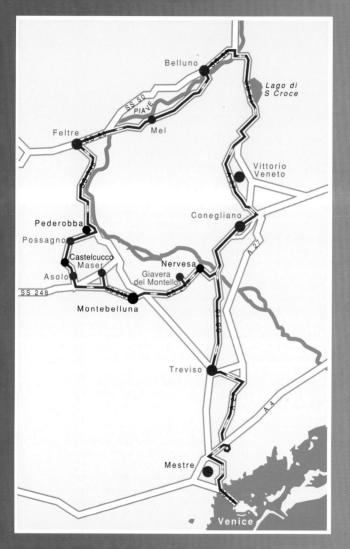

Treviso - Asolo

278 km. *2 days - leaving early, with a stop for lunch at Lago di S Croce, an overnight stay in Feltre and lunch the following day in Giavera.*

Leave Venice in the direction of Mestre (8 km) and follow the signs for the A 4 to Trieste. Once on the A 4, take the first turn-off on the right. This brings you onto the A 27. Turn off at the Treviso Sud exit.

32 km - Treviso (see **A-Z**). Faithful mainland satellite of the Venetian Republic from the 14thC onwards. Despite extensive bombing in 1944 this medieval city has managed to retain its charm. Leave on the SS 13.

60 km - Conegliano. The birthplace of the painter Cima da Conegliano (1460-1518), whose superb *Christ's Baptism* can be seen at San Giovanni in Bragora in Venice. His house, at Via Cima 19, is open to the public (summer 1600-1800, winter 1500-1700). The Gothic Duomo (14th-15thC) in Via XX Settembre is also worth visiting. It contains an impressive *Virgin and Saints* by Cima. Return to the A 27.

79 km - Vittorio Veneto (see **A-Z**). The town consists of two distinct parts - Ceneda below and Serravalle above. Follow the SS 51 for 30 km then turn left onto the SS 50 for a further 8 km. Stop along the way for lunch in the Lago di S Croce region where there are plenty of good restaurants to choose from.

117 km - Belluno (see **A-Z**). A beautiful, Renaissance mountain town lying at the confluence of the Ardo and Piave rivers. Take the road along the left bank of the Piave leading to Feltre via Mel.

132 km - Mel. A charming old town whose main square, the Piazza Umberto, is lined with attractive 16th and 17thC houses.

140 km - Feltre (see **A-Z**). Famous for the 16thC frescoes which adorn the facades of many of its houses. Take the SS 348 towards Treviso and follow it for 22 km. Turn off at Pederobba for Possagno.

182 km - Possagno. Birthplace of the most famous Italian sculptor of the neoclassical age, Antonio Canova (1757-1822). You can visit his house (summer 0900-1200, 1500-1800 Tues.-Sun.; winter 0900-1200, 1400-1900 Tues.-Sun.; L. 2500.) and the Tempio del Canova (summer 0800-1200, 1400-1900; winter 0800-1200, 1330-1700), which houses his tomb (sculpted by the artist himself). Follow the road south through Castelcucco.

190 km - Asolo (see **A-Z**). A delightful little town overlooked by its

Asolo

historically significant fortress. Take the SS 248 towards Montebelluna and then the turning on the left for Maser.

200 km - Maser. The most important sight here, in fact an absolute must, is the Villa Barbaro just north of the town (summer 1500-1800 Tues., Sat., Sun.; winter 1400-1700 Tues., Sat., Sun.; L. 4000). Built in 1555, it is perhaps the most impressive of Palladio's rural villas. The first floor is lavishly decorated with frescoes by Veronese. Return to the SS 248 going to Montebelluna (8 km). From here follow the SS 248 for 9 km before turning left.

219 km - Giavera del Montello. Situated at the foot of the Montello mountain and surrounded by picturesque countryside (where raging battles were fought at the end of World War I). The town is famous for the abundance and quality of the mushrooms which grow in the region. For lunch, try the Trattoria Agnoletti at Via Vittoria 121 (Wed.-Sun., Mon. am; closed 1-10 July) before carrying on to Nervesa and turning south onto the SS 13.

246 km - Treviso. Rejoin the A 27 from here, then take the A 4 to Mestre (24 km). Follow the SS 11 to return to Venice (8 km).

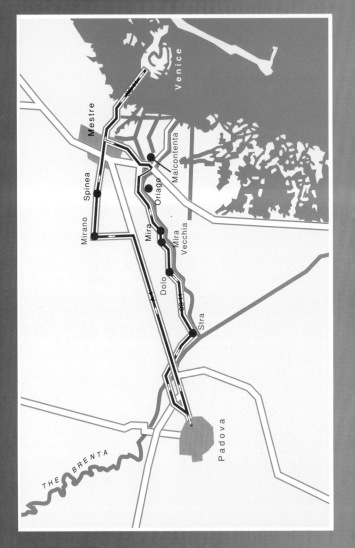

The Brenta

78 km. *1 day. A similar trip can be made by boat (see* **Burchiello***).*

From Venice, take the SS 11 to Mestre and head towards Ravenna on the SS 309 (la Romea). Immediately after the roundabout turn left for Malcontenta.

5 km - Malcontenta. Here you can visit one of the most famous of the Palladian villas, the Villa Foscari (1571), also known as *La Malcontenta* or 'The Discontented' (Mar.-Oct. 0900-1200, Tues., Sat. and first Sun. of the month). According to legend the villa is named after the owner's wife who was confined here for her unfaithfulness. In reality, the villa takes its name from the village itself, which, for obscure reasons, has been called this since 1431! Drive along the SS 11 in the direction of Oriago (3 km) and keep going towards Mira. A kilometre before it on the right is the Villa Foscari Widman (1719), which has beautiful late-Baroque frescoes (0800-1200, 1400-1800 Tues.-Sun.; L. 6000.).

21 km - Mira Vecchia. The site of the Palazzo Foscarini, home of Lord Byron between 1817 and 1819. The elegant Villa Venier Contarini (1612) is just beyond the town, to the right. Carry straight on.

25 km - Dolo. Turn right at the church and, beyond the canal, you will find the Villa Ferretti Angeli, which is now a school (gardens: 0730-1930 summer, 0730-1600 winter). Return to the main road and keep going in the same direction.

31 km - Stra. The Villa Pisani Nazionale (1736-1756) is the most sumptuous of all the villas along the Brenta. Bought by Napoleon in 1807, it was subsequently owned by the Hapsburgs. There are 200 rooms, many of which were lavishly decorated by 18thC Venetian painters such as G. B. Tiepolo. Hitler and Mussolini had their first encounter here in 1934. Don't miss the delightful garden and its famous maze (0900-1330 Tues.-Sun.; L. 3000.). Continue along the SS 11.

43 km - Padova. A university town rich in important works of art and architecture (see **A-Z**). Return to Venice from here along the A 4. If you have time turn off at the Dolo-Mirano exit for Mirano.

67 km - Mirano. The Villa Belvedere in the centre of town has a particularly beautiful park (summer 0900-1200, 1430-2000; winter 0900-1200, 1400-1700). Drive towards Mestre, passing through Spinea, on the Via Miranese, then return to Venice (19 km) on the SS 11.

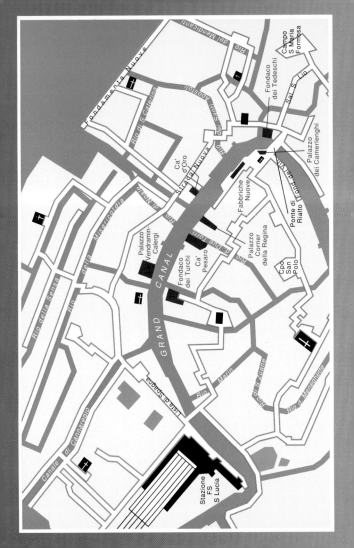

Station - Rialto

A trip down the Grand Canal in a gondola or on a vaporetto (line 1 or 4) is an excellent way to see some of the city's most important buildings.

FONDACO DEI TURCHI Line 1, S Marcuola.
An early 13thC building (one of the oldest in Venice) which takes its name from the Turkish merchants who lived and worked here in the 17th-18thC. Now houses the Museo di Storia Naturale (See MUSEUMS 2*). See* **Fondaco***.*

PALAZZO VENDRAMIN-CALERGI Line 1, S Marcuola.
A superb Renaissance palace designed by Codussi (see **A-Z***), where Richard Wagner died in 1883. Today it is a casino. See* **NIGHTLIFE***.*

CA' PESARO Line 1, S Stae.
It took 50 years to build this luxurious Baroque palace for the Pesaro family. It now contains two important museums. See MUSEUMS 2*,* **A-Z.**

PALAZZO CORNER DELLA REGINA Line 1, S Stae.
An imposing palace built by Domenico Rossi (1724-27) on the site of the birthplace of Caterina Cornaro (see **A-Z***), the unfortunate Venetian Queen of Cyprus.*

CA' D'ORO Line 1, Ca' d'Oro.
A stunning mid-15thC Gothic palace. The name derives from the lavish gold-leaf decoration that originally covered its facade. See MUSEUMS 2*,* **A-Z***.*

FABBRICHE NUOVE Line 1, 4, Rialto.
25 arches line the ground floor of this Renaissance building designed by Sansovino (see **A-Z***), which is now the Court of Assizes.*

FONDACO DEI TEDESCHI Line 1, 4, Rialto.
This fondaco *(see* **A-Z***) originally housed German merchants and had frescoes by Titian and Giorgione on its facade. Today it is the main post office.*

PALAZZO DEI CAMERLENGHI Line 1, 4, Rialto.
Built in the 16thC as the offices of the chamberlains of the Republic, the ground floor was then used as a prison.

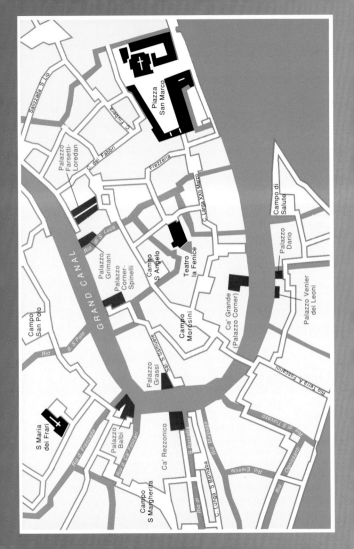

Rialto - S Marco

PALAZZO FARSETTI-LOREDAN Line 1, 4, Rialto.
Elegant 13thC Veneto-Byzantine twin palaces. Now the Town Hall.

PALAZZO GRIMANI Line 1, 4, Rialto.
The Court of Appeal lies behind the magnificent facade of this massive Renaissance palazzo designed by Sanmicheli in 1556.

PALAZZO CORNER-SPINELLI Line 1, S Angelo.
The first Renaissance-style palazzo to be built in Venice (1490-1510), it was designed by Mauro Codussi (see A-Z).

PALAZZO BALBI Line 1, 4, S Tomà.
A beautiful late-Renaissance palace by Alessandro Vittoria (completed 1590). Since the early 1970s it has been the seat of the regional government.

PALAZZO GRASSI Line 1, Ca' Rezzonico and *traghetto* to S Samuele; 2, S Samuele.
A huge neoclassical structure built by Massari in the mid 18thC. See A-Z.

CA' REZZONICO Line 1, Ca' Rezzonico; 2, S Samuele and *traghetto* to Ca' Rezzonico.
A 17thC palace with a lavish interior, built by Longhena (see A-Z). It houses the fascinating Museo del Settecento. See MUSEUMS 3, A-Z.

CA' GRANDE (PALAZZO CORNER) Line 1, S Maria del Giglio.
Built by Sansovino (see A-Z) for the Corner family (see A-Z) in the mid 16thC. It now serves as the Prefecture of Venice.

PALAZZO VENIER DEI LEONI Line 1, 2, 4, Accademia.
Only one level of this curious building was ever completed. See MUSEUMS 3, WALK 1, A-Z, Raccolta Peggy Guggenheim.

PALAZZO DARIO Line 1, 2, 4, Accademia.
Built in the mid 15thC for Giovanni Dario, a diplomat who served the Republic in Constantinople. Has one of the most charming facades in Venice. Note also the tall, typically Venetian, chimneys.

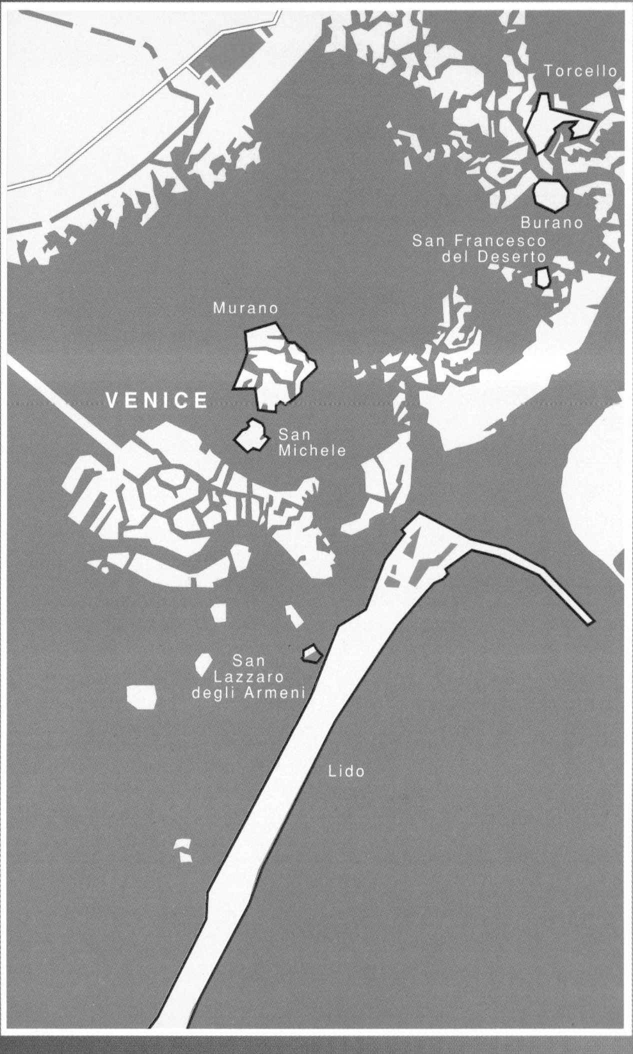

Torcello

Burano

San Francesco
del Deserto

Murano

VENICE

San
Michele

San
Lazzaro
degli Armeni

Lido

LIDO 1.5 km east.
Line 1, 2, 4, 6, 11 from Riva degli Schiavoni. Takes 15 min.
*A long, narrow sandy island which reached the height of its popularity as a bathing resort in the 19thC. See **A-Z**.*

MURANO 1.5 km north.
Line 5, 12 from Fondamenta Nuove. Takes 10 min.
*Centre of the world-famous glass industry since the 13thC. See **A-Z**.*

BURANO 9 km north east.
Line 12 from Fondamenta Nuove. Takes 45 min.
*Here you'll find charming multi-coloured fishermen's houses, as well as the lace for which the island is renowned. See **A-Z**.*

TORCELLO 10 km north east.
Line 12 from Fondamenta Nuove. Takes 50 min.
*The site of one of the lagoon's earliest settlements (6thC). Its 7thC cathedral attracts many visitors. See **A-Z**.*

SAN MICHELE 1 km north.
Line 5 from Fondamenta Nuove. Takes 5 min.
*Location of the city cemetery (the tombs include that of Stravinsky) and one of the lagoon's most striking churches, San Michele in Isola. See **A-Z**.*

SAN FRANCESCO DEL DESERTO 8 km north east.
Regular service from near S Martino Church on Burano. Takes 20 min.
St Francis is said to have stopped here on his way back from the Holy Land in the early 13thC. The monastery was built shortly afterwards (0900-1100, 1500-1730; donation expected).

SAN LAZZARO DEGLI ARMENI 1.3 km south east.
Line 10, from Riva degli Schiavoni. Takes 10 min.
Home of the Armenian community since 1717. Books were printed here in no less than 36 languages. The museum displays some of the books and mementoes of Byron, who came here to study Armenian (1500-1700 Tues., Sun.). Look out for some famous signatures in the visitors' book.

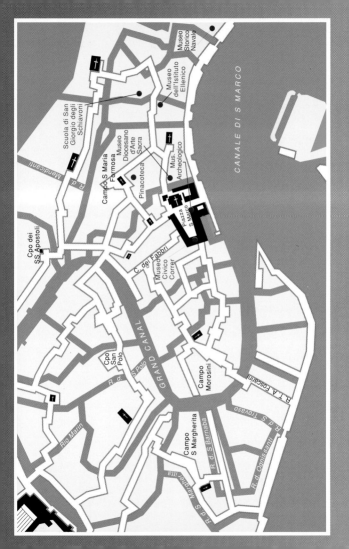

Central & East

MUSEO CIVICO CORRER Piazza S Marco 52.

• 1000-1600 Sun., 0930-1230 Mon., Wed.-Sat. Line 1, 2, 4, S Marco, S Zaccaria. • L. 3000.

Principal civic museum of Venetian art and history. See **A-Z**.

SCUOLA DI SAN GIORGIO DEGLI SCHIAVONI Calle dei Furlani, Castello 8259/A.

• 1000-1230, 1530-1800 Tues.-Sat.; 0930-1230 Sun. Line 1, 2, 4, S Zaccaria. • L. 3000.

Founded by the Dalmatian community. Houses a magnificent series of paintings by Carpaccio (best viewed between 1130-1230 when the light is good). See **WALK 2, A-Z**.

PINACOTECA Palazzo Querini-Stampalia, Campiello Querini, Castello 4778.

• 1000-1230 Tues.-Sun. Line 1, 2, 4, S Zaccaria. • L. 5000.

Venetian paintings from the 14th-18thC, as well as furniture and tapestries.

MUSEO DIOCESANO D'ARTE SACRA Fondamenta S Apollonia, Castello 4312.

• 1030-1230 Mon.-Sat. Line 1, 2, 4, S Zaccaria. • Free.

Displays works on loan from churches undergoing restoration. See **WALK 2**.

MUSEO ARCHEOLOGICO Libreria Vecchia, Piazzetta S Marco 17.

• 0900-1400 Tues.-Sat.; 0900-1300 Sun. Line 1, 2, 4, S Marco. • L. 2000.

A large archeological collection including Greek and Roman statues.

MUSEO STORICO NAVALE Riva degli Schiavoni, Castello 2148.

• 0900-1300 Mon.-Fri.; 0900-1200 Sat. Line 1, Arsenale. • L. 1000.

Fascinating exhibits revealing the full extent of the Venetian Republic's naval power. See **WALK 2, A-Z**.

MUSEO DELL'ISTITUTO ELLENICO C. dei Greci, Castello 3412.

• 0930-1230, 1400-1800 Mon., Wed.-Sat.; 0930-1230 Sun. Line 1, 2, 4, S Zaccaria. • L. 3000.

A most unusual display of 14th-18thC Byzantine icons. See **WALK 2**.

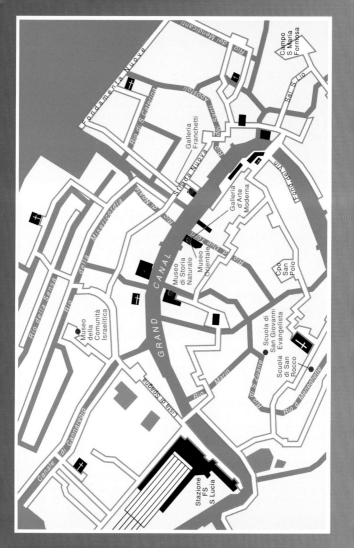

Central & North

SCUOLA GRANDE DI SAN ROCCO Campo S Rocco, S Polo.
•0900-1300 (and 1530-1830 Sat., Sun.). Line 1, 4, S Tomà. •L. 5000.
It took Tintoretto 23 years to complete the magnificent series of paintings which adorn this 16thC scuola. See **WALK 2, A-Z**.

SCUOLA DI SAN GIOVANNI EVANGELISTA Campiello di S Giovanni, S Polo.
•1500-1800 Mon.-Sat. Line 1, 4, S Tomà.
15thC building with a grand staircase by Codussi (see **A-Z***). The oratory contains a splendid reliquary which holds a fragment of the True Cross.*

GALLERIA FRANCHETTI Calle Ca' d'Oro, Cannaregio.
•0900-1400 Tues.-Sat.; 0900-1300 Sun. Line 1, Ca' d'Oro. •L. 2000.
Exhibits an outstanding collection of European art. See **Ca' d'Oro**, **A-Z**.

GALLERIA D'ARTE MODERNA Ca' Pesaro, S Croce 2078.
•0900-1600 Tues.-Sat; 0930-1230 Sun. Line 1, S Stae. •L. 3000
An impressive collection of modern art, including works by Bonnard, Chagall, de Chirico, Kandinsky, Klimt, Matisse and Rodin. See **Ca' Pesaro**.

MUSEO ORIENTALE Ca' Pesaro, Calle Pesaro, S Croce.
•0900-1400 Tues.-Sat.; 0900-1300 Sun. Line 1, S Stae. •L. 2000.
An intriguing display of military items, costumes and works of art from Japan, China and other parts of the Far East. See **Ca' Pesaro**.

MUSEO DELLA COMUNITÀ ISRAELITICA Campo Ghetto Nuovo, Cannaregio.
•1015-1230 (and 1500-1800 summer) Mon.-Fri., 1000-1230 Sun. and Jewish hol. Guided tours: 1100, 1200, 1500, 1600. Line 1, S Marcuola; 5, Ponte di Guglie. •L. 2000.
Exhibits items used in Jewish rituals during the 17th-19thC. See **Ghetto**.

MUSEO DI STORIA NATURALE Fondaco dei Turchi, S Croce 1730.
•0900-1300 Tues.-Sun. Line 1, S Stae. •L. 3000.
A natural history museum housing one of the largest dinosaur skeletons in the world. See **GRAND CANAL 1**.

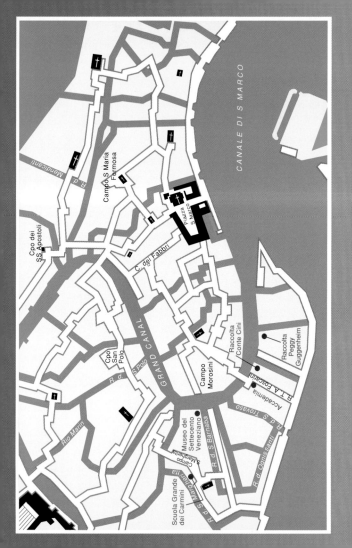

CANALE DI S MARCO

Mendicanti

R. d.

Cpo dei
SS. Apostoli

Campo S Maria
Formosa

C. dei Fabbri

Piazza
S Marco

Cpo
San Polo

R. d.

S. Polo

GRAND CANAL

Campo
Morosini

Rio Marin

Raccolta
Conte Cini

Raccolta Peggy
Guggenheim

Accademia

R. d. S. Trovaso

R. d. A. Foscarini

Museo del
Settecento
Veneziano

Campo
S. Margherita

R. d. S Barnaba

R. d. Ognissanti

Scuola Grande
dei Carmini

R. d. S. Maurizio
Ca

South

ACCADEMIA Campo della Carità.

•0900-1400 (1300 Sun.). Line 1, 2, 4, Accademia. •L. 4000.
This is the most comprehensive collection of Venetian paintings in the world. The collection includes many undisputed masterpieces by such artists as Gentile and Giovanni Bellini, Carpaccio, Giorgione and Titian. See **WALK 1**, **A-Z**.

MUSEO DEL SETTECENTO VENEZIANO Ca' Rezzonico.

•1000-1600 Mon.-Thurs., Sat., 0900-1200 Sun. Line 1, Ca' Rezzonico.
•L. 3000.
18thC paintings, sculpture and furniture gathered from various Venetian houses and arranged in this splendid Baroque palazzo. See **GRAND CANAL 2, Ca' Rezzonico A-Z**.

RACCOLTA PEGGY GUGGENHEIM Palazzo Venier dei Leoni, Calle S Cristoforo.

•1100-1800 Wed.-Mon. (2100 Sat.). Line 1, 2, 4, Accademia.
•L. 5000 (free 1800-2100 Sat.).
A priceless collection of modern art assembled by the great American connoisseur. Includes works by Picasso, Kandinsky, Dalì and Pollock. See **GRAND CANAL 2, WALK 1, A-Z**.

RACCOLTA CONTE CINI Campo S Vio.

•1400-1900 Tues.-Sun. (June-Oct.). Line 1, 2, 4, Accademia.
•L. 4000.
Conte Vittorio Cini's small but precious collection of Venetian and Tuscan masterpieces includes works by Botticelli, Piero di Cosimo and Filippo Lippi. Also exhibits illuminated manuscripts, drawings and furniture. See **WALK 1**.

SCUOLA GRANDE DEI CARMINI Campo dei Carmini.

•0900-1200, 1500-1800 Mon.-Sat. Line 1, Ca' Rezzonico; 5, 8, S Basilio. •L. 2000.
This Baroque building is particularly noteworthy for containing a marvellous series of frescoes by G. B. Tiepolo, which are counted among his finest works. See **Carmini, Tiepolo**.

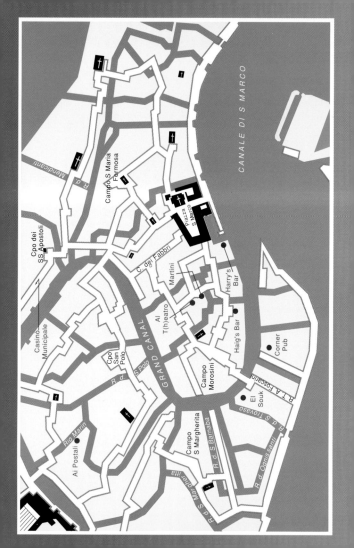

HARRY'S BAR Calle Vallaresso, S Marco 1323.
•1030-2300 Tues.-Sun. Closed Jan. Line 1, 2, 4, S Marco. •Expensive.
Sample the famous Bellini champagne and peach juice cocktails and savour the atmosphere of a bar frequented by film stars, writers and politicians. One of Hemingway's favourite watering holes.

HAIG'S BAR Campo del Traghetto, S Marco 2477.
•1000-0200 Thurs.-Tues. Line 1, S Maria del Giglio. •Moderate.
Ideal for night owls. Normally quieter, and cheaper, than Harry's Bar.

AI POSTALI Fondamenta Rio Marin, S Croce 821.
•1800-0200 Wed.-Mon. •Moderate.
A small intimate bar that is popular with young people. Frequently has live music.

CORNER PUB Calle della Chiesa, Dorsoduro 684.
•0700-0200 Wed.-Mon. Line 1, 2, 4, Accademia. •Moderate.
A small but lively pub with a predominantly English-speaking clientele.

AL T(H)EATRO Campo S Fantin, S Marco 1916.
•0800-2400 Tues.-Sun. Closed Nov. Line 1, S M. del Giglio. •Moderate.
A popular bar with a terrace on the elegant Campo S Fantin.

MARTINI Campo S Fantin, S Marco 2007.
•2200-0330 Wed.-Mon. Closed Nov.-Jan. Line 1, S M. del Giglio.
•Expensive.
A stylish nightclub with a lively disco and occasional live music.

EL SOUK Calle Corfù, Dorsoduro 1056A.
•2130-0200. Line 1, 2, 4, Accademia. •Moderate.
A small disco with a usually packed dance floor, and a good restaurant.

CASINÒ MUNICIPALE Apr.-Sept.: Lungomare G. Marconi, Lido.
Line 1, 2, 4, 6, 11, S M. Elisabetta. Oct.-Mar.: Palazzo Vendramin-Calergi, Strada Nuova, Cannaregio 2040. Line 1, S Marcuola.
Two of the most glamorous casinos in the world.

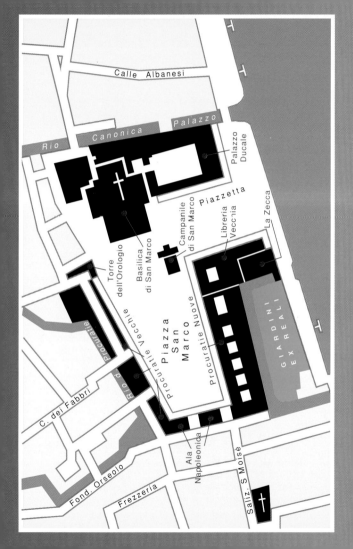

BASILICA DI SAN MARCO
•0930-1700 Mon.-Sat., 1400-1700 Sun.
An astonishing 11thC Byzantine structure. See BASILICA DI S MARCO, **A-Z**.

PALAZZO DUCALE (DOGES' PALACE)
•0830-1600 (1400 winter). •L. 5000.
The seat of Venetian power from the 9thC until the fall of the Republic in 1797. See DOGES' PALACE, **A-Z**.

CAMPANILE DI SAN MARCO
•1000-1930. •L. 3000.
Ascend the tower for unrivalled views of the city and lagoon. See **A-Z**.

TORRE DELL'OROLOGIO Merceria dell'Orologio 147.
•0900-1200, 1500-1700 Tues.-Sat., 0900-1200 Sun.
A beautiful Renaissance clock tower designed by Codussi. See **A-Z**.

PROCURATIE VECCHIE
A Veneto-Byzantine-style building dating from 1512-26. Originally the offices of the State Procurators, the Republic's administrators.

PROCURATIE NUOVE
An extension of the Procuratie Vecchie. It was used by the Procurators until 1797, when Napoleon made it his 'royal' palace.

ALA NAPOLEONICA
Napoleon had the existing buildings demolished to make way for this neo-classical structure. Now the Museo Correr. See MUSEUMS 1, **Museo Correr**.

LIBRERIA VECCHIA (SANSOVINIANA)
Built to one of Sansovino's (see **A-Z***) most successful and influential designs, but not completed until after his death in 1591. See* MUSEUMS 1.

LA ZECCA
This was the city mint and one of Sansovino's first commissions (begun in 1536). The mint was closed down in 1870.

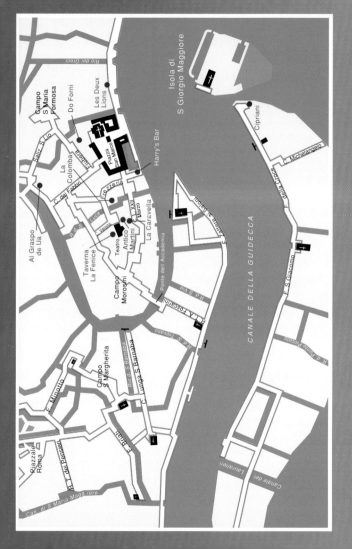

Expensive

HARRY'S BAR Calle Vallaresso, S Marco 1323.
• 2300 (last orders) Tues.-Sun. Closed Jan. Line 1, 2, 4, S Marco.
A world-famous establishment catering for those with refined palates and substantial wallets. Try the carpaccio *(thin strips of raw beef).*

CIPRIANI Campo Nani e Barbaro, Giudecca 10.
• 2400 (closing time). Closed Nov.-15 Mar. Line 5, 8, Zitelle.
Perhaps the most sophisticated restaurant in Venice. Lovely gardens.

ANTICO MARTINI Campo S Fantin, S Marco 1983.
• Thurs.-Mon., Wed. eve. Closed Nov.-Mar. Line 1, S M del Giglio.
Exclusive restaurant with an extensive à la carte menu.

LES DEUX LIONS Londra Palace Hotel, R. Schiavoni, Castello 4171.
• Wed.-Mon. (Thurs. in summer). Line 1, Arsenale; 1, 2, 4, S Zaccaria.
A plush restaurant which serves exquisite nouvelle cuisine-style seafood.

AL GRASPO DE UA Calle dei Bombuseri, S Marco 5094.
• Fri.-Sun. Closed Christmas hol. Line 1, 4, Rialto.
Much frequented by Venetians since it opened almost 100 years ago.

TAVERNA LA FENICE Campiello la Fenice, S Marco 1938.
• Tues.-Sat., Mon. eve. Line 1, 2, 4, S Marco; 1, S Maria del Giglio.
Situated on a charming little square. Delicious pasta and exquisite truffles.

DO FORNI Calle dei Specchieri, S Marco 457.
• Fri.-Wed. Line 1, 2, 4, S Zaccaria.
Large trattoria with Orient Express-style decor and an impressive menu.

LA COLOMBA Piscina di Frezzeria, S Marco 1665.
• Thurs.-Tues. Line 1, S Maria del Giglio.
Excellent restaurant renowned both for its seafood and its arty decor.

LA CARAVELLA Calle Larga XXII Marzo, S Marco 2397.
• 0100 (closing time) Fri.-Tues., Thurs. eve. Line 1, 2, 4, S Marco.
Venetian specialities served in the sophisticated setting of the Saturnia Hotel.

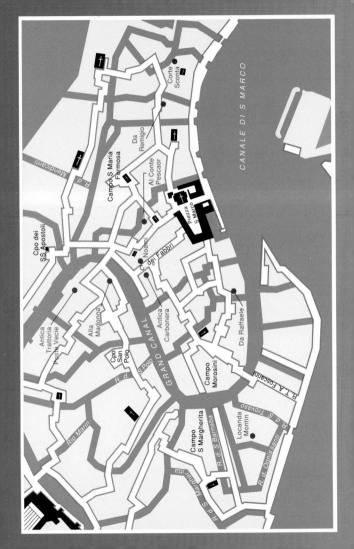

Moderate

AL CONTE PESCAOR Piscina S Zulian, S Marco.
•Tues.-Sat., Mon. eve. Line 1, 2, 4, S Marco; 1, 4, Rialto.
Serves some of the best grilled fish in Venice. Friendly service.

ALLA MADONNA Calle della Madonna, S Polo 594.
•Thurs.-Tues. Line 1, 4, Rialto.
Large seafood restaurant. Try the squid in black sauce with polenta.

DA RAFFAELE Fondamenta delle Ostreghe, S Marco 2347.
•Fri.-Wed. Closed Christmas hol. Line 1, S Maria del Giglio.
Exquisite Venetian specialities served on a pleasant terrace by the canal.

ANTICA TRATTORIA POSTE VECIE Pescheria, S Polo 1608.
•Wed.-Mon. Line 1, 4, Rialto.
A typically Venetian trattoria with a magnificent interior.

CORTE SCONTA Calle del Pestrin, Castello 3886.
•Tues.-Sat. Closed Jan., 17 July-17 Aug. Line 1, Arsenale.
Stylish decor and a delightful garden. Inventive, wholesome cuisine.

ANTICA CARBONERA Calle Bembo, S Marco 4648.
•Wed.-Mon. Line 1, 4, Rialto.
Interesting decor, attentive service and delicious yet unpretentious dishes.

NOEMI Calle dei Fabbri, S Marco 909.
•Mon.-Sat. Closed Dec., Jan. Line 1, 2, 4, S Marco.
Superb Italian cuisine. Try Sogliola alla Casanova *(sole in white wine sauce).*

LOCANDA MONTIN Fondamenta di Borgo, Dorsoduro 1147.
•Thurs.-Mon., Tues. lunchtime. Line 1, 2, 4, Accademia.
A fashionable trattoria hung with interesting paintings. Has a pleasant garden.

DA REMIGIO Salizzada dei Greci, Castello 3416.
•Wed.-Sun., Mon. lunchtime. Closed Christmas hol. Line 1, Arsenale.
A busy seafood restaurant popular with locals.

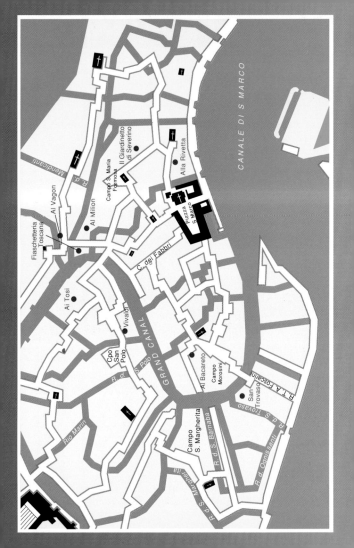

Budget

IL GIARDINETTO DI SEVERINO Salizzada Zorzi, Castello 4928.
•Sun.-Fri. Line 1, 2, 4, San Zaccaria
Venetian cuisine and magnificent ceilings. You can also eat alfresco.

VIVALDI Calle Madonnetta, S Polo 1457.
•Tues.-Sat., Sun. lunchtime. Line 1, San Silvestro.
Family-run trattoria patronized by locals for its hearty Venetian specialities.

ALLA RIVETTA Salizzada San Provolo, Castello 4625.
•Tues.-Sun. Closed July. Line 1, 2, 4, S Zaccaria.
A small trattoria behind the Basilica di S Marco. Excellent value for money.

AI TOSI Campo Beccarie, S Polo 1586.
•Tues.-Sun. Line 1, 4, Rialto.
Typical seafood restaurant that remains almost exactly as it was last century.

AL BACARETO Salizzada S Samuele, S Marco 3447.
•Mon.-Fri., Sun. lunchtime. Closed Aug. Line 1, S Angelo; 2, S Samuele.
Lively trattoria near the Palazzo Grassi, frequented by students and artists.

FIASCHETTERIA TOSCANA Salizzada S Giovanni Crisostomo, Cannaregio 5719.
•Wed.-Mon. Closed 1-15 July. Line 1, 4, Rialto.
An extremely pleasant restaurant and wine bar on two floors.

AL MILION Calle Corte del Milion, Cannaregio 5841.
•Thurs.-Tues. Closed Aug. Line 1, 4, Rialto. Behind S G. Crisostomo.
Venetian delicacies. Marco Polo is said to have lived in this building.

SAN TROVASO Fondamenta Priuli, Dorsoduro 1016.
•Tues.-Sun. Closed July. Line 1, 2, 4, Accademia.
An unpretentious trattoria offering delicious pasta and tasty pizzas.

AL VAGON Sottoportego del Magazen, Cannaregio 5597.
•Wed.-Mon. Closed Nov. Line 1, 4, Rialto.
Good-value seafood served on a terrace on the lovely Rio dei SS Apostoli.

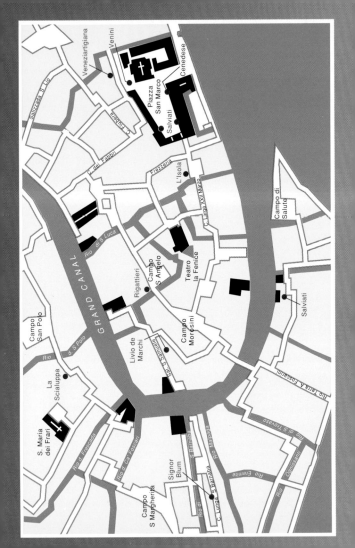

Arts & Crafts

VENEZIARTIGIANA Calle Larga S Marco, S Marco 412/3.
• Closed Mon. am. Line 1, 2, 4, S Zaccaria, S Marco.
A consortium of Venetian craftsmen. Glassware, jewels, paper and masks.

SALVIATI Piazza S Marco 70 and 110, S Marco.
• Closed Mon. am. Line 1, 2, 4, S Marco.
Renowned glassmaker. The furnace and showroom are at Calle del Bastion 194.

CENEDESE Piazza S Marco 153/a, S Marco.
• Closed Mon. am. Line 1, 2, 4, S Marco.
Renowned for its glorious mirrors, vases and drinking glasses.

VENINI Piazzetta dei Leoni, S Marco 314.
• Closed Mon. am. Line 1, 2, 4, S Marco.
Ultra-modern designs in glassware, tableware, lamps and vases.

L'ISOLA Campo S Moise, S Marco 1468.
• Closed Mon. am. Line 1, 2, 4, S Marco.
Some of the finest contemporary designs in tableware and vases.

RIGATTIERI Calle dei Frati, S Marco 3532/36.
• Closed Mon. am. Line 1, 2, 4, Accademia.
Fancy silverware, ceramics, pottery and tableware. Good value for money.

LIVIO DE MARCHI Salizzada S Samuele, S Marco 3157/a.
• Closed Sat. Line 1, S Samuele.
Superb wooden trompe l'oeil items including tablecloths and hanging coats.

LA SCIALUPPA Calle dei Saoneri, S Polo 2695.
Line 1, 4, S Tomà.
Models and jigsaw puzzles of some of the city's prettiest buildings.

SIGNOR BLUM Calle Lungo S Barnaba, Dorsoduro 2864.
Line 1, Ca' Rezzonico.
Intriguing range of hand-made wooden objects and toys.

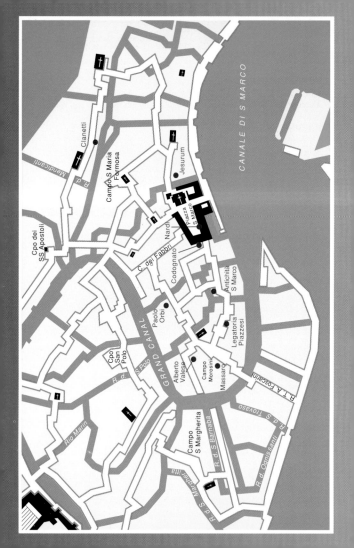

Arts & Crafts

ANTICHITÀ SAN MARCO Calle XXII Marzo, S Marco 2407.
Line 1, 2, 4, S Marco; 1, S Maria del Giglio.
Venetian paintings, furniture and sculptures, and precious curios.

NARDI Piazza S Marco 69-71, S Marco.
• Closed Mon. Line 1, 2, 4, S Marco.
Renowned jeweller famous for his Otellos - black jewel-encrusted heads.

CODOGNATO Calle dell'Ascensione, S Marco 1295.
• Closed Mon. am. Line 1, 2, 4, S Marco.
Interesting modern jewellery as well as superb antique pieces.

LEGATORIA PIAZZESI Campiello della Feltrina, S Marco 2511/c.
• Closed Mon. am. Line 1, S Maria del Giglio.
Hand-printed paper. Excellent designs from the neighbouring workshop.

PAOLO ORBI Calle della Mandola, S Marco 3653.
• Closed Mon. am in winter. Line 1, S Angelo.
Hand-made marbled paper used to cover a wide range of stationery items.

ALBERTO VALESE Salizzada S Samuele, S Marco 3135.
• Closed Mon. am in winter. Line 1, S Angelo; 2, S Samuele.
The oldest surviving specialist in multicoloured marbled paper.

MASSARO Calle Vetturi, S Marco 2934.
Line 1, 2, 4, Accademia.
You will see Massaro's masks on sale everywhere, but it's cheaper to buy them here at his workshop.

CLANETTI Barbaria delle Tole, Castello 6657.
Line 5, Ospedale Civile; 1, 2, 4, S Zaccaria.
Master mask-makers catering for all Carnival enthusiasts.

JESURUM Ponte Canonica, S Marco 4310.
• Closed Mon. am in winter. Line 1, 2, 4, S Zaccaria.
Superb display of lacework and embroidered linen in a magnificent setting.

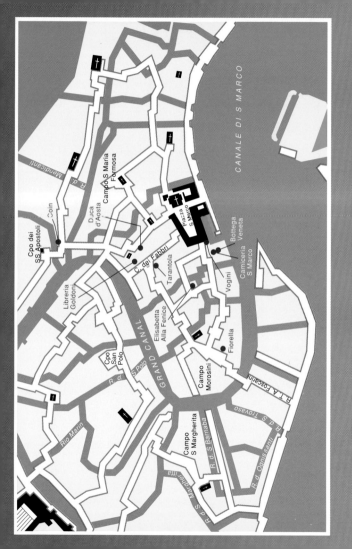

Gifts & Souvenirs

BOTTEGA VENETA Calle Vallaresso, S Marco 1337.
• Closed Mon. am in winter. Line 1, 2, 4, S Marco.
The classic Italian look in bags, shoes and elegant silk scarves.

VOGINI Calle dell'Ascensione, S Marco 1291, 1301, 1305.
• Closed Mon. am in winter. Line 1, 2, 4, S Marco.
Leather goods - from the tiniest purse to the largest suitcase.

COIN Salizzada S G. Cristostomo, Cannaregio 5788.
Line 1, 4, Rialto.
The biggest clothes shop in Venice, housed in a 15thC palace. Great value.

ELISABETTA ALLA FENICE Campo San Fantin, S Marco 1996.
• Closed Mon. am in winter. Line 1, S Maria del Giglio, S Angelo.
An upmarket boutique selling mainly Italian designs (Valentino, Krizia, etc).

FIORELLA Campo Morosini, S Marco 2800.
• Closed Mon. am. Line 1, S M. del Giglio, S Angelo.
Stylish clothes made with Fortuny-style fabrics.

CAMICERIA SAN MARCO Calle Vallaresso, S Marco 1340.
Line 1, 2, 4, S Marco.
Choose from a superb range of materials and have a shirt, blouse or pyjamas made to measure - it only takes a day!

DUCA D'AOSTA Merceria dell'Orologio, S Marco 4922 and 4945.
• Closed Mon. am in winter. Line 1, 2, 4, S Marco.
Classical, elegant menswear. Also carries a small range of women's fashions.

LIBRERIA GOLDONI Calle dei Fabbri, S Marco 4742.
• Closed Mon. am in winter. Line 1, 4, Rialto; 1, 2, 4, S Marco.
Large general bookshop with a good foreign book department.

TARANTOLA Campo S Luca, S Marco 4268.
• Closed Mon. am in winter. Line 1, 4, Rialto.
Old and new guidebooks, art books and foreign titles (mainly in English).

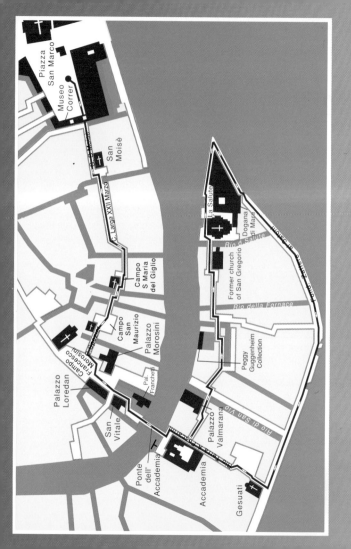

San Marco - Salute

2 hr - *excluding visits to museums, galleries and churches.*

Leave the Piazza San Marco and pass under the arches of the Museo Civico Correr (see **MUSEUMS 1, A-Z**). Cross over the Calle Seconda dell'Ascension into the Salizzada San Moisè opposite, which is lined with prestigious shops and leads to the small Campo San Moisè, dominated by the grand Baroque facade of its church (see **CHURCHES 3**) but somewhat spoilt by the drearily modern Hotel Bauer Grünwald.
Cross the canal and follow the Calle Larga XXII Marzo, taking you past the Venice Stock Exchange (on your right) to the Campo Santa Maria del Giglio, sometimes known as the Campo S Maria Zobenigo after the Baroque church on the north side of the square. The church was built by Sardi (1681-3) following instructions left by the racketeering diplomat Antonio Barbaro, who died in 1679.
Continue in the same direction and cross over two more canals and you arrive in the delightful Campo San Maurizio, around which are a number of antique shops and the Church of S Maurizio. The Calle Piovan leads from here into the narrow Calle del Spezier, taking you into the vast Campo Francesco Morosini, also known as Campo S Stefano. Morosini was a Venetian military commander who led a highly destructive raid on the city of Athens in 1667 (which obliterated, among other things, part of the Parthenon). On his return he was made Doge. His palace stands on your left opposite the beautiful Palazzo Loredan (now the Institute of Venetian Arts, Letters and Sciences). Go to the south side of the square and you will pass (on your right) the former church of San Vitale, which is now an art gallery. To your left is the Palazzo Franchetti, which was modified in the 19thC by Giorgio Franchetti, a former owner of the Ca' d'Oro (see **A-Z**).
Cross the Grand Canal on the Ponte dell'Accademia - a wooden bridge originally built as a temporary structure in 1932 - and admire the view. Dominating the right bank of the canal, as you look towards San Marco, is the church of La Salute (see **A-Z**). The former church of La Carità (Charity), with its monastery and *scuola*, stands on the other side of the bridge. Since the beginning of the 19thC it has housed the Accademia (Academy of Fine Art) and its famous museum (see **MUSEUMS 3, A-Z**) - allow yourself at least two or three hours to visit it.

Ponte dell'Accademia

Go left around the Accademia and take the Calle Nuova Sant'Agnese on the left. Before you come to the first bridge you will see, again on your left, the Palazzo Valmarana, housing the delightful Cini collection (see **MUSEUMS 3**).

Cross the bridge and you will see the small church of San Vio on your right, and St George's (Anglican services every Sun. - see **Religious Services**) on your left. Take the Calle della Chiesa from here, and then carry straight on along Fondamenta dei Leoni before turning left into the Calle S Cristoforo, where you will find the entrance to the Raccolta (Collection) Peggy Guggenheim (see **MUSEUMS 3, A-Z**).

Cross over yet another bridge and turn left into the Calle Barbaro leading into the Calle del Bastion, where you can visit Cenedese's glass workshop at No. 175 before continuing straight on past the former church of San Gregorio. Cross the next bridge and you arrive at La Salute (see **CHURCHES 3, A-Z**), Longhena's (see **A-Z**) masterpiece. Skirt around the Dogana di Mare (Maritime Customs Offices) to find yourself on the Zattere, the wide sunny quays giving superb views of the island of Giudecca (see **A-Z**). A 15 min walk along the Zattere leads you to the church of the Gesuati (see **CHURCHES 3, A-Z**).

Turn right into Rio Terrà A. Foscarini, which takes you back to the Ponte dell'Accademia. From here retrace your steps to S Marco.

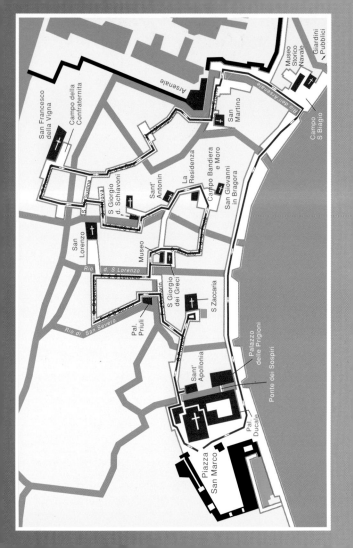

Castello

2hr 30 min - *excluding visits to museums, galleries and churches.*

Leave the Piazza S Marco on the Piazzetta dei Leoni to the left of the
Basilica, and take the Calle Canonica alongside the Palazzo Patriarcale.
Follow the street round the back of the palace. From the bridge there is
an unimpeded view of the Bridge of Sighs (see **Ponte dei Sospiri**),
which connects the Doges' Palace (see **DOGES' PALACE**, **Palazzo Ducale**)
to the Palazzo delle Prigioni (formerly known as the Prigioni Nuove -
New Prisons - or the Prigioni della Paglia - Prisons of Straw, but now
closed). The small Fondamenta S Apollonia on the other side of the
canal leads to the Scuola di Sant'Apollonia, now the Museo Diocesano
d'Arte Sacra (see **MUSEUM 1**). Don't miss the superb Jesurum lacework
showroom just beside the *scuola* (see **SHOPPING 2**).
Following the Rughetta Sant'Apollonia and the Salizzada San Provolo,
you come to San Zaccaria, one of the oldest churches in the city (see
CHURCHES 1, A-Z). Return to the Campo San Provolo and turn right into
the Calle San Provolo, which becomes the Fondamenta dell'Osmarin,
then take the Ponte del Diavolo on your left. Stop and admire the
facade of the Gothic Palazzo Priuli (15thC) standing on your left, before
carrying straight on and then turning left into the Fondamenta di S
Severo. Go right, into Borgoloco S Lorenzo, and you will see the beautiful, unfinished facade of the church of San Lorenzo directly ahead of
you, in a shady *campo* on the other side of the canal. The church is
now used for temporary exhibitions and cultural events. Walk along the
Fondamenta di San Lorenzo, cross the third bridge and turn right
towards San Giorgio dei Greci and the small Museo dell'Istituto
Ellenico (see **MUSEUMS 1**).
Retrace your steps, then take the Calle della Madonna and turn right
behind the church into Calle dei Greci (which becomes Calle Bosello).
Go left into Calle dietro la Pietà and cross the bridge to reach one of
the most attractive *campi* in Venice, the Campo Bandiera e Moro,
named after two heroes of the 19thC struggle for Italian independence.
On the right is the church of San Giovanni in Bragora (see **CHURCHES 1**)
and on the left is the beautiful Gothic Palazzo Gritti-Badoer, now the
pensione La Residenza. Leave the *campo* on the Salizzada S Antonin to
the right of La Residenza, and turn right at the church of Sant'Antonin.

Arsenale

Continue along the Fondamenta dei Furlani to reach the Scuola di S
Giorgio degli Schiavoni, its interior superbly decorated with frescoes by
Carpaccio (see **MUSEUMS 1**, **A-Z**). Cross the bridge, turn right, and head
along the Fondamenta degli Schiavoni to the next bridge. Cross it, and

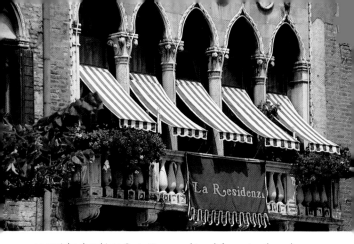

go straight ahead into Corte Nuova and turn left, passing through a narrow passageway. Turn left again into Salizzada S Giustina, and then right into Calle del Fontego. Cross the bridge, continue along the Calle del Te Deum, then turn right into Calle S Francesco, which takes you to the church of S Francesco della Vigna (see **CHURCHES 1**).

The route to the Arsenale from here leads through a maze of picturesque, deserted alleys, narrow streets and nameless *corte*. From the Campo della Confraternita (to the right of the church), cross the canal and follow the Salizzada San Francesco, the Salizzada de le Gate and the Calle va al Ponte dei Scudi. Turn left into Calle del Mandolin to Campiello dei Due Pozzi, then right into Calle delle Muneghette, and right again along the Fondamenta Penini until you reach the small church of San Martino with its delightful Renaissance facade by Sansovino (see **A-Z**). Take the Fondamenta di Fronte to the left of the church and you arrive in front of the gates of the Arsenale (see **A-Z**), where two enormous stone lions guard the entrance. Cross the bridge, turn right, and walk alongside the Rio dell'Arsenale until you reach Campo S Biagio, site of the Museo Storico Navale (see **MUSEUMS 1**, **A-Z**). From here you can either walk back to the Piazza S Marco along the quays or take the vaporetto (1, Arsenale). Alternatively, you can extend your walk down to the Giardini Pubblici and the island of Sant'Elena, from where you can return to S Marco by vaporetto 1 or 2.

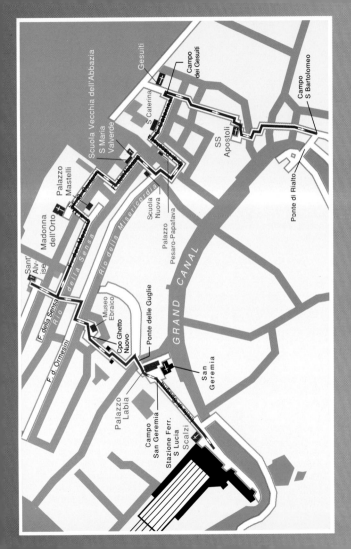

Cannaregio

2 hr - excluding visits to museums, galleries and churches.

Begin at the station. To the right of the station you will see the heavy facade of the Scalzi, completed by Sardi in 1680. The church was badly damaged by an Austrian bomb in 1915, which partly destroyed the nave and a superb fresco by G. B. Tiepolo (fragments are in the Accademia). Take the wide Lista di Spagna ahead of you, leading to the vast Campo San Geremia. The Palazzo Labia, now owned by the RAI (the Italian equivalent of the BBC), stands on the opposite side of the square. The Labia were one of the wealthiest families in Venice in the 17thC. They gained notoriety through one member of the family who, during interminable parties, used to throw his silver and gold plates out of the window shouting *'L'abbia o non l'abbia, sarò sempre Labia'* - 'Whether I have it or have it not, I'll always be a Labia'! To the right is the 13thC church of San Geremia (restored in the 18thC). It contains the remains of St Lucy, which were formerly housed in the church demolished to make way for the station.

Leave the *campo* on the Salizzada S Geremia off its north side. Cross the Ponte delle Guglie, turn left along the canal, and take the Sottoportego del Ghetto on the right, which leads to the Campiello della Scuola, where two synagogues face the Scuola Spagnola and the Scuola Levantina. Continue along the Calle del Ghetto Vecchio into the Campo Ghetto Nuovo, the centre of an area which gave us the word 'ghetto' (see **Ghetto**). With six to eight floors, the buildings here are the tallest in Venice. On the right is the Museo della Comunità Israelitica (see **MUSEUMS 2**). Leave the Ghetto by crossing the Austrian-built Ponte de Ghetto Novo over the Rio della Misericordia. Turn right onto the Fondamenta degli Ormesini and then left into the Calle della Malvasia, which leads across the Rio della Sensa and (becoming the Calle di Capitello) the Rio di Sant'Alvise to the church of Sant'Alvise. This sober-facaded church houses a beautiful *Calvary*

Ghetto

by G. B. Tiepolo (in the presbytery), but unfortunately is only open for
early-morning Mass. Note that there are no *campi* in this part of
Cannaregio; instead local people gather on the pleasant south-facing
quays. Back on the Calle del Capitello, turn left onto the Fondamenta
della Sensa, becoming the Fondamenta dei Mori, and left again into the
Campo dei Mori. Note the statues on the wall of the main *palazzo*

here. They are said to depict the three Mastelli brothers, Levantine tradesmen who fled from the Peloponnese in 1112 and settled in Venice. One of the statues stands on the wall of the house Tintoretto occupied for the last 20 years of his life (No. 3399). At the far end of the *campo* stands the charming church of Madonna dell'Orto (see **CHURCHES 2, A-Z**).

Take the Fondamenta Gasparo Contarini and, on the other side of the canal, you will see the facade of the brothers' palace, the Palazzo Mastelli, embellished with a bas-relief depicting merchants following their laden camels. From the bridge at the end of the quay there is a fine view over the northern part of the lagoon, with the islands of San Michele, Venice's cemetery, and Murano directly opposite you (see **LAGOON, A-Z**). Cross the bridge and take the Corte Vecchia, then turn left onto the Fondamenta dell'Abbazia. The Scuola Vecchia dell'Abbazia and the small church of S Maria Valverde (13th C) stand at the end of the quay. When the brotherhood was transferred to the Scuola Nuova (built by Sansovino - see **A-Z -** in 1538) on the other side of the canal in the 16th C, the Scuola Vecchia was taken over by a community of silk spinners.

Cross the wooden bridge and walk alongside the Scuola Nuova, pausing to admire the 15thC Gothic facade of the Palazzo Pesaro-Papafava, then cross the Ponte della Misericordia and turn right into the Fondamenta S Felice. Cross the next bridge and go through the Sottoportego dei Preti, opening into the Calle della Racchetta. At the end of the *calle* cross the Rio di S Caterina, then turn right. Pass by the church of S Caterina (now a school) and walk along the Fondamenta Zen leading into the Campo dei Gesuiti, an attractive, usually deserted, *campo*. The Gesuiti church here is one of the most beautiful Baroque churches in Italy (see **CHURCHES 2, A-Z**).

Cross the Ponte dei Gesuiti and follow the Salizzada Seriman and the Calle del Spezier. Take the Rio Terrà dei SS Apostoli and the Rio Terrà dei Franceschi, before turning right into the Calle Larga dei Proverbi, and right again to the church of SS Apostoli on its shell-shaped *campo*. Leaving the *campo*, cross the bridge and take the Sottoportego Falier, the Calle del Dolfin and the Salizzada S G. Crisostomo which leads to the Campo S Bartolomeo. The Rialto lies to your right (Lines 1, 4).

Accademia: The Accademia delle Belle Arti, located in the former church, convent and *scuola* of La Carità, was founded in the mid-18thC. Many of the gallery's works of art were donated by academicians, while other paintings came from private collections and churches which had closed down. Since the 19thC, acquisitions have been funded by the State.

Without doubt this is the most comprehensive collection of Venetian art anywhere - almost every room contains at least one undisputed masterpiece. The arrangement of the rooms is more or less chronological, allowing the visitor to trace the development of Venetian painting from the 14thC to the 18thC.

Among the highlights of the collection are works by Giovanni Bellini (rooms 2, 4, 5), Gentile Bellini (make sure you see *The Procession in Piazza S Marco* in room 20), Carpaccio (in particular the *St Ursula* series, room 21), Giorgione (the famous and enigmatic *The Tempest* is in room 5), Lotto (note the poignant *Portrait of a Young Man in His Study* in room 7), Tintoretto (the superb *St Mark* cycle is in room 10), Titian (rooms 9, 10, 24), and Veronese (rooms 10, 11).See **MUSEUMS 3, Bellini, Carpaccio, Giorgione, Tintoretto, Titian, Veronese**.

Accidents and Breakdowns: If you have an accident, follow the usual procedure of exchanging names, addresses and insurance details. To contact the police or other emergency services, dial 113. If someone is injured and you are held responsible, insist on contacting your embassy or consulate as soon as possible (see **Consulates**).

You should carry a red warning triangle with you at all times. These can be hired for a nominal sum from the ACI (Automobile Club Italiano) offices at the frontier. If you have a breakdown, place the warning triangle 50 m behind your car and then seek help. Motorways have emergency telephones at one kilometre intervals. Dial 116 for assistance from the ACI. If you have petrol coupons some of your repairs may be carried out free of charge. See **Driving**.

Accommodation: Tends to be very expensive in Venice, and for most of the year it is advisable to book in advance. If you arrive without accommodation, try the hotel booking services at the station (expect a long queue), the airport, or on the Piazzale Roma (Mon.-Sat.). If nothing is available in Venice itself, you should be able to find somewhere to stay in Mestre (see **A-Z**).

Prices for a double room in Venice range from L. 50,000 per night, in *locande* or *pensione* (inns), to L. 300,000-600,000 per night in luxury hotels, but a reasonable two-star hotel costs approx. L. 100,000. See **Camping and Caravanning, Youth Hostels.**

Airport: The nearest international airport is Marco Polo Airport, 13 km north of the city. It has all the usual facilities, including a bar, restaurant, duty-free shop, post office, toilets and an efficient hotel booking office.

You can reach Venice from the airport by:

Vaporetto (water bus) - probably the most picturesque and enjoyable method. Departures roughly coincide with flight arrivals. It takes about 40 min to get to the Lido and about 50 min to reach San Marco.

Bus - ATVO coaches meet both domestic and international flights. The journey to Piazzale Roma takes about 20 min and costs L. 4000.

Water taxi - for those who wish to travel in comfort and style. Costs approx. L. 90,000 for four people, plus luggage, going to the Lido, and L. 80,000 to San Marco.

Taxi - Approx. L. 20,000 to the Piazzale Roma.

Arsenale: A massive fortress-like structure originally built in the 12thC as a centre for the Republic's shipbuilding activities. The name derives from the Arabic *dar sina'a*, meaning 'house of construction'. The Arsenale eventually employed a highly skilled workforce of some 16,000 men who, it was said, could turn out a  fully-equipped warship in 12 hours! Nowadays the Arsenale is a military zone and, unfortunately, is closed to the public. You can, however, admire the exterior, with its impressive 15thC entrance arch surmounted by the winged lion of St Mark and guarded by two stone lions looted from Piraeus in the 17thC. You can also pass through the Arsenale on vaporetto (water bus) No. 5, a trip which allows you a brief glimpse of the interior's crumbling grandeur. See **WALK 2**.

Asolo: 60 km north west of Venice. Pop: 7000. Trains to Bassano del Grappa, then local bus (takes 3 hr). A picturesque town in the Asolean hills, renowned for the beauty of the surrounding countryside and for the quality of its hotels and restaurants. The town centre is composed of narrow medieval streets lined with elegant arcades and charming houses decorated with exterior frescoes. The Duomo in the Piazza Maggiore contains paintings by Lorenzo Lotto and Jacopo Bassano; while the Museo Civico in the Loggia del Capitano has mementoes of such figures as Caterina Cornaro (see **A-Z**), who lived in exile here from 1489, and Eleonora Duse, as well as a variety of interesting paintings (0930-1200, 1600-1900 Tues.-Sat.). A massive fortress, La Rocca, stands above the town, commanding a fine view. See **EXCURSION 1**.

Baby-sitters: There is no official baby-sitting service in Venice but your hotel may be able to recommend someone. Private baby-sitters charge approximately L. 15,000 an hour.

Baroque: A style which prevailed in the art and architecture of the 17thC and is characterized by an uninhibited use of elaborate decoration. Notable Baroque buildings in Venice include the Ca' Rezzonico (see **GRAND CANAL 2, A-Z**), the Ca' Pesaro (see **GRAND CANAL 1, A-Z**) and the church of the Gesuiti (see **CHURCHES 2**).

Basilica di San Marco: The first building to bear this name was built in the 9thC to house the remains of St Mark, which had been smuggled to Venice from Alexandria by a group of Venetian merchants. It was used by doges as a private chapel until it was almost completely destroyed by fire in 976. The church was rebuilt, but soon replaced by a far more elaborate edifice as befitted (by then) such a great power as the Venetian Republic. Merchants returning from abroad were ordered to bring precious objects to adorn the new building, while the most talented artists and craftsmen available were employed to further embellish the magnificent structure. The Byzantine style of the Basilica

Basilica di S Marco

reflects the city's strong links with the East during the 11th and 12thC. Even after relations with Byzantium deteriorated, precious objects continued to arrive from the East, many of them plundered in the crusades of the early 13thC. The great onion-shaped domes of the Basilica were added in the 13thC and the building has changed relatively little since then. The breathtaking interior defies description. The play of light on the brilliant decoration reveals new glories every hour of the day. See **BASILICA DI S MARCO**. For opening times see **PIAZZA SAN MARCO**.

Bellini, Gentile (1429-1507): Elder son of the highly regarded painter Jacopo Bellini (1400-70/71). Gentile was extremely successful during his lifetime and his skill was recognized both abroad (by the Holy Roman Emperor, who awarded him a knighthood in 1469) and in Venice itself, where he was made official painter to the Republic in 1474. His accurate depictions of contemporary civic and religious events are treasured both as masterpieces of narrative painting and as valuable historical documents. His work can be seen in the Accademia (see **MUSEUMS 3**, **A-Z**) and the Museo Correr (see **MUSEUMS 1**).

Bellini, Giovanni (c.1430-1516): Younger son of Jacopo Bellini. Giovanni learned a great deal from his father and also from his brother-in-law, Andrea Mantegna, but gradually developed a highly individual style. His subjects are usually traditional - Madonnas, saints, etc - but his mastery of the new medium of oil painting, and his ability to integrate figures and landscape, helped him infuse these subjects with a humanity and a lyricism which none of his contemporaries could match. Some of the many major works by Bellini to be found in Venice are housed in the Accademia (see **MUSEUMS 3**, **A-Z**) and the church of the Frari (see **CHURCHES 2**, **A-Z**).

Belluno: 108 km north of Venice. Pop: 36,000. Three or four trains a day from Venice (takes 2 hr). A popular winter sports centre also notable for its fine Renaissance buildings. Outstanding amongst these is the Palazzo dei Rettori in the Piazza del Duomo, an extraordinary Venetian-style building begun in 1491. The 11thC Torre Civica, which was originally part of a castle, stands next to it. The Duomo (cathedral), built in the 16thC by Tullio Lombardo, has a fine Baroque campanile and a remarkable interior containing paintings by Jacopo Bassano and Palma il Giovane. The 15thC Gothic church of Santo Stefano is also worth visiting. A curious Roman sarcophagus stands beside it. See **EXCURSION 1**.

Best Buys: Venice and the islands in its lagoon are famous for a number of crafts. Look out for the following in particular:
Glass - mirrors, drinking glasses, ornaments, jewellery. The most sought-after glassware comes from Murano (see **A-Z**).
Masks - papier-maché and leather carnival masks make highly unusual gifts.
Paper - hand-made marbled paper and hand-printed paper.
Wood - balsa-wood models of Venetian buildings and hand-made jigsaws.

Lace - both modern and traditional designs. Burano (see **A-Z**) lace is particularly famous. Other local products include leather goods, silk, ceramics and prints. See **SHOPPING**, **A-Z**.

Biennale: One of the most important events in the visual arts calendar. As its name suggests, this major exhibition is biennial and takes place in June during even-numbered years. The 30 or so pavilions displaying modern art from all over the world are spread around the Giardini Napoleonici di Sant'Elena, the Arsenale (see **A-Z**) and the Zattere (see **A-Z**).

Brenta Canal: The Brenta Canal begins south of Padova and runs to Fusina on the coast to the south of Venice. Although parts of the canal have been rather spoilt by industrial development and pollution, a trip along the Brenta is still one of the most pleasant and interesting excursions that can be made from Venice. The superb villas along the banks of the canal, many of them built by Palladio (see **A-Z**), are of particular interest. See **EXCURSION 2**.

Bridge of Sighs: See **Ponte dei Sospiri**.

Budget:	Breakfast in hotel	from L. 5000.
		L. 10,000 in two-star hotel.
	Vaporetto ticket	L. 1700.
	Museum ticket	L. 800-5000.
	Lunch	L. 15,000-100,000.
	Ice-cream	L. 1000-10,000.
	Coffee	L. 800-5000.

Dinner	from L. 15,000.
Wine	from L. 4000 (per bottle).
Brandy	from L. 3000 (per glass).
Beer	from L. 2500 (per glass).
Cinema ticket	from L. 8000.
Theatre ticket	L. 17,000-80,000.

See **Accommodation**.

Burano: Burano consists of four small islands separated by canals and linked by bridges. The first settlers came here in the early 11thC and made their living principally from fishing the waters of the lagoon. Even today fishing is still an integral part of life on Burano, and the fishing boats and brightly-coloured fishermen's houses are characteristic of the island. The lace industry, for which Burano is renowned, dates back to the 16thC. The Scuola dei Merletti (Lacemaking School) and its museum, on the Piazza Galuppi, are open to the public (0900-1800; hol. 1000-1600; L. 2000). Don't leave the Piazza Galuppi without visiting the church of San Martino with its leaning campanile and, inside, a magnificent *Crucifixion* by G. B. Tiepolo. See **LAGOON**.

Burchiello: A boat which makes regular trips from the Pontile Giardinetti, San Marco, to Padova via the Brenta Canal (departing 0900 Tues., Thurs., Sun.; arriving 1930; returning by bus from the Piazzale Boschetti every half hour till 2200). A return ticket including lunch at the Il Burchiello restaurant in Oriego costs L. 105,000 (L. 73,000 without lunch). Book in advance at the CIT travel agency in Piazza San Marco. See **EXCURSION 2.**

Buses: Buses for various mainland destinations depart from the Piazzale Roma near the station. Services are generally efficient, comfortable and reasonably priced. Contact the tourist office (see **Tourist Information**) or the bus station for timetables and details of excursions, prices, etc. See **Transport.**

Byzantine: An architectural style which originated in Byzantium and is characterized by large domes, rounded arches, minarets and mosaic decoration. Many buildings in Venice, particularly those which predate the 16thC, are built in a Venetian version of this style, normally referred to as 'Veneto-Byzantine'.

Ca': An abbreviation of the word *casa*, meaning 'house'. Traditionally, the large palaces built for the leading Venetian families were all referred to as *ca'* (as in Ca' Pesaro), while the only building which warranted the grander title of *palazzo* was the Palazzo Ducale (Doges' Palace). Nowadays most of the palaces are referred to as *palazzi*, although in one or two cases the name *ca'* has stuck. The versions adopted in this book are those most commonly used today.

Ca' d'Oro: A magnificent example of Venetian-Gothic architecture. Built in the 1420s for the procurator Marino Contarini, its facade was originally embellished with gold leaf, giving rise to its name, meaning 'house of gold'. In the 19thC, the Russian Prince Alexander Troubetskoy made a present  of the palace to the ballerina Marina Taglioni. Unfortunately, she proceeded to spoil the exterior of the building by demolishing the stairway

and front porch. Some of the damage was repaired by a subsequent owner, Count Giorgio Franchetti, who then donated the building and his art collection to the State. The palace is open to the public. See **GRAND CANAL 1, MUSEUMS 2, Galleria Franchetti.**

Cameras and Photography: Most well-known brands of film and photographic equipment are widely available in Venice, but films tend to be expensive, so stock up before you come. Developing is also costly. Photography is generally permitted in churches and museums, but special permission is required for using a tripod or taking pictures of particular works of art. Find out at the individual museum, church or gallery whether you are allowed to use a flash there.

Campanile di San Marco: The first tower on this site was begun in the 9thC, but the tower assumed its present form in 1514 when it was rebuilt after an earthquake. Over the centuries it served a variety of purposes - it was a watchtower, a lighthouse, and even an observatory (Galileo demonstrated his telescopes here to Doge Leonardo Donà in 1609). In the Middle Ages one form of punishment meted out by the

Republic involved hanging prisoners in a cage from the south side of the tower. On 14 July 1902 the structure collapsed without warning but, amazingly, the only victim was the caretaker's cat. The building reopened ten years later having been painstakingly rebuilt. A lift now takes visitors to the top of the 100 m high tower, from where they can enjoy magnificent views over the city and the lagoon. The *loggetta* at the foot of the campanile was erected in the mid-16thC, and served as a popular meeting place for Venetian nobles. The graceful structure is built of red marble from Verona and white Istrian stone and is decorated with bronze statues by Sansovino (see **A-Z**).

Camping and Caravanning: You cannot camp within Venice itself or on the Lido, but there are a number of well-equipped sites within easy reach of the city. The closest are near Mestre and on the Cavallino Peninsula (Line 12, 14, 15 from Venice). They cost approx. L. 25,000 per night for two people, a car and a tent. For full details, contact the tourist office in Venice (see **Tourist Information**) or the Italian Tourist Office in Britain.

Canaletto (1697-1768): Antonio Canal's detailed paintings of his native city are famous throughout the world but, surprisingly, very few of his works are to be found in Venice. This is because his paintings were phenomenally popular with contemporary tourists, and consequently most of them ended up in foreign collections. There are however works in the Accademia (see **MUSEUMS 3**, **A-Z**) and in the Museo Settecento Veneziano (see **MUSEUMS 3**, **A-Z**).

Cannaregio: See **CITY DISTRICTS, WALK 3**.

Ca' Pesaro: An elaborate Baroque building built for the Pesaro family. It was begun by Longhena (see **A-Z**) and completed by Antonio Gaspari in 1710. The palace remained the property of the Pesaro family until 1830 and was later bequeathed to the State. The two richly ornate facades are particularly impressive. Inside are two important museums, the Galleria Internazionale di Arte Moderna and the Museo Orientale (see **MUSEUMS 2**). See **GRAND CANAL 1**.

Ca' Rezzonico: A massive Baroque palace designed by Longhena (see **A-Z**) for the Bon family. Begun in 1667, it was only completed in 1756, by which time it had passed to the Rezzonico family, wealthy bankers who spent extravagantly on lavish decorations and furnishings for their palace. In the 19thC it became the home of the poet Robert Browning, who died here in 1889. It now houses the Museo del Settecento Veneziano (see **A-Z**). See **GRAND CANAL 2, MUSEUMS 3.**

Car Hire: There are a number of car-hire offices in the Piazzale Roma and at the airport. Most firms will allow you to deliver the car to another Italian city when you are finished with it, and some of them have special weekend deals. To hire a car in Italy you must have held a licence for at least one year and be over 21 years of age. Unless you pay by credit card you will have to leave a large deposit.

Carmini: The 17thC Gothic church of Santa Maria del Carmelo was originally founded in the 14thC by the Carmelite order. The building has an imposing brick facade and a fine campanile. The interior of the church has recently been restored. The church's works of art include paintings by Cima da Conegliano and Lorenzo Lotto. There are some impressive frescoes in the nearby *scuola*, including G. B. Tiepolo's *Virgin in Glory,* which pleased the monks so much that they made the artist an honorary member of the Carmelite order. See **CHURCHES 3.**

Carnevale: The annual carnival was an important feature of Venetian life from medieval times to the end of the 18thC, when Napoleon abolished it. From St Stephen's Day (26 Dec.) up to Shrove Tuesday, before they endured the austerities of Lent, the Venetians made the most of their social life and freedoms. People from all walks of life, and all parts of Europe, wore masks and fancy dress, played practical jokes, attended bullfights and boxing matches, and watched acrobats and performing animals. The Mayor of Venice revived the carnival in the 1970s, and once again it is the social highlight of the year.

Carpaccio, Vittore (1450/55-1525/26): Another great Venetian painter, noted for his meticulously detailed paintings of Venetian life

Ca' Rezzonico

and his mastery of perspective. He frequently worked for the *scuole* (see **Scuola**) and his magnificent series of paintings depicting the lives of St George, St Tryphonius and St Jerome can still be seen in the Scuola di S Giorgio degli Schiavoni (see **MUSEUMS 1**, **A-Z**). Other works by him are housed in the Accademia (see **MUSEUMS 3**, **A-Z**) and the Museo Correr (see **MUSEUMS 1**, **A-Z**).

Castelfranco Veneto: 45 km north west of Venice. Pop: 40,000. Trains every 2 hr (takes 1 hr). The birthplace of the painter Giorgione (see **A-Z**) whose *Madonna* can be seen in the 18thC Duomo on the Piazza S Liberale, which also houses paintings and frescoes by Palma il Giovane and Veronese. Giorgione's house stands nearby and is open to the public (0930-1230, 1500-1830 Sat., Sun.). The old part of the town centre is surrounded by majestic 12thC walls.

Chemist's: Chemist's generally keep normal shop hours (see **Opening Times**), but they also operate a rota system, so that at least one chemist is open outside normal hours. Details are displayed in every chemist's window under the sign *Farmacie di Turno*. The same list is published in the local newspaper *Il Gazzettino*.

Children: The novelty of the vaporetti is sure to amuse children and a short trip on a gondola can be both fun and instructive. Otherwise, try taking children up the Campanile (see **A-Z**), to the Naval Museum (see **Museo Storico Navale**) to see the marvellous model ships, or to the Museo di Storia Naturale (see MUSEUMS 2) to see the dinosaur skeletons. Make sure you include one or two stops along the way for a scrumptious ice cream at one of the city's excellent cafés.

Chioggia: 25 km south of Venice. Pop: 55,000. Line 11 from Riva degli Schiavoni; Bus SIAMIC from Piazzale Roma every 30 min (takes 50 min). A pleasant fishing port reached by a causeway from the mainland. Until 1379, when the city was destroyed by the Genoese, it was the second most important town in the province.

Climate: The best times for visiting Venice are spring and autumn when the temperature is mild and there isn't too much rain. Winter can be cold and wet, and snow is not unheard of (average temp. 4°C). In summer the temperature can rise to 38°C (average 28°C). In winter, during heavy rain, the city is regularly flooded, and knee-length boots (for sale all over the city) become *de rigueur.*

Codussi, Mauro (1440-1504): A highly talented architect born in Bergamo in Lombardy. Little is known about his life prior to his arrival in Venice. His first work in the city was the beautiful Renaissance church of S Michele in Isola (1469-77 - see LAGOON, **San Michele**). Other works include the Palazzo Vendramin-Calergi (see GRAND CANAL 1), the Torre dell'Orologio (see PIAZZA S MARCO, **A-Z**) and, his last work, the church of S Giovanni Crisostomo (see CHURCHES 2).

Complaints: If you feel that you have been unfairly treated or overcharged, report it to the Tourist Office (see **Tourist Information**) who will investigate the matter. More serious complaints should be taken to the police (see **A-Z**).

Consulates:
Great Britain - Dorsoduro 1051. Tel: 5227207.

United States - Largo Donegani 1, Milan. Tel: (02) 652841.
Canada - Via Vittore Pisani 19, Milan. Tel: (02) 652600.
Australia - Via Turati 40, Milan. Tel: (02) 6598727.
New Zealand - Via Zara 28, Rome. Tel: (06) 44.02928.

Conversion Charts:

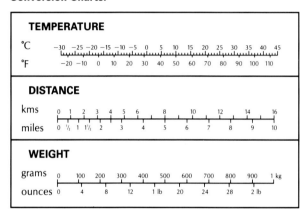

TEMPERATURE

°C −30 −25 −20 −15 −10 −5 0 5 10 15 20 25 30 35 40 45
°F −20 −10 0 10 20 30 40 50 60 70 80 90 100 110

DISTANCE

kms 0 1 2 3 4 5 6 8 10 12 14 16
miles 0 ½ 1 1½ 2 3 4 5 6 7 8 9 10

WEIGHT

grams 0 100 200 300 400 500 600 700 800 900 1 kg
ounces 0 4 8 12 1 lb 20 24 28 2 lb

Cornaro, Caterina (1454-1510): Venetian aristocrat who married the King of Cyprus at the age of 17. She was deposed and exiled to Asolo, where she was visited by poets and scholars. See **EXCURSION 1**.

Corner: One of the most powerful aristocratic families in the history of the city. They provided a number of doges, including Marco (1365-8), Giovanni I (1625-9), Francesco (1656) and Giovanni II (1709-22). No fewer than 16 *palazzi* in Venice are named after the family. The name Corner is a Venetian corruption of Cornaro (see **A-Z**).

Crime and Theft: Crime is not widespread in Venice but you should still leave all your valuables in the hotel safe and take care to carry wallets or purses in a secure pocket. Keep a separate list of the numbers of your traveller's cheques and a note of your passport number. If you are the victim of a robbery or any other crime, go to the police (see **A-Z**) immediately, and retain a copy of their report for insurance purposes. In the case of stolen traveller's cheques, also inform the office where they were issued. In the case of a stolen passport, inform your consulate (see **A-Z**) at once. See **Emergency Numbers, Insurance.**

Currency: The Italian monetary unit is the lira (pl. lire), often written as L. before the amount. Coins in circulation are worth 10, 20, 50, 100, 200 and 500 lire. Notes are in denominations of 1000, 2000, 5000, 10,000, 50,000 and 100,000 lire. Due to the scarcity of anything smaller than a L. 50 coin, you may be given sweets, matches or *gettoni* (telephone tokens) in place of small change.

Doge: The elected head of government during the period of the Republic. The word derives from the Latin *dux*, meaning 'leader'. The first doge was elected by the inhabitants of the city in 726. From the earliest days of the Republic, however, the Venetians were quick to rise up against any doge who seemed to abuse his power. In 976, for example, the citizens razed the Doges' Palace to the ground and killed the extremely corrupt Doge Pietro Candiano. Subsequently, more and more restrictions were placed on the doge's activities, and numerous committees were appointed to dilute his power. By the 16thC the government was structured, in simple terms, as follows:
The 480 (later almost 1700) members of the *Maggior Consiglio* (Great Council), for the most part Venetian noblemen, were responsible for electing the doge and other members of government. The doge himself attended their meetings with his small coterie of close advisers known as the *Signoria*, without whom he was unable to act. He also had a *Collegio* (Cabinet) who oversaw all state affairs and the legislation introduced by the 120 members of the Senate (also elected by the *Maggior Consiglio*). A separate and extremely powerful body, the *Consiglio dei Dieci* (Council of Ten), kept a close eye on the activities of the doge and the other members of the government. Eventually the position of doge, although a great honour, was little more than that of a

figurehead. Despite this, the Venetian system of government was much admired both in Italy and abroad, and it served its citizens well. The last doge was Lodovico Manin, who surrendered the city to Napoleon in 1797.

Doges' Palace: See DOGES' PALACE, **Palazzo Ducale.**

Dorsoduro: See CITY DISTRICTS.

Drinks: The local red and white wines are extremely palatable, while Prosecco, the white sparkling wine produced in Conegliano, is outstanding. Ask for the house wine (*vino della casa*) when eating in inexpensive restaurants as it is normally good value. The water, though safe

to drink, has a rather unpleasant taste of chlorine, and Venetians usually prefer to drink mineral water. A wide variety of beers, fizzy drinks and fruit juices is available in the city. For something stronger try *grappa*, a strong northern-Italian spirit made from grape skins. If you ask for a coffee (*un caffé*) you will receive an espresso, a small, strong black coffee. If you want a little milk in it, order it *macchiato*. A cappuccino is an espresso with frothy milk, covered with a sprinkling of chocolate. If you prefer a plain white coffee, ask for a *caffellatte*. Tea is served in most restaurants and hotels, mainly to tourists.

Driving: Third party insurance is obligatory when driving in Italy. Make sure you have your driving licence and car registration papers and that you are displaying a national identity sticker. You must also carry a red warning triangle in case of breakdowns (see **Accidents and Breakdowns**). Petrol coupons (giving discounts on petrol) and motor-way vouchers (for use at motorway tolls) are available for foreign motorists bringing their cars into the country (but not if you hire a car there). These are available from automobile associations in your own country or Automobile Club Italiano (ACI) branches at border crossings (not within Italy). The ACI offers reciprocal membership to members of affiliated foreign automobile associations and will come to your aid if you have a breakdown.

Drive on the right-hand side of the road and remember that traffic from the right has priority unless otherwise indicated. Italian roads are generally good, especially motorways - although you have to pay a toll to use them. If caught speeding, you may have to pay the fine on the spot.

Drugs: All drugs are illegal and there are severe penalties for offenders. Contact your embassy or consulate (see **A-Z**) if you are arrested for a drugs-related offence.

Electricity: 220 volts. Two-pin plugs are used and adaptors are available in Italy and in the UK.

Emergency Numbers:

Police	113.
Carabinieri	112.
Ambulance	5230000 (Blue Cross motorboat service).
Fire brigade	115.
Breakdown service	116.

See **Crime and Theft, Health, Lost Property Offices, Police**.

Events:

Feb.: Carnevale (see **A-Z**).

Ascension: Festa de la Sensa, commemorating the day on which the doge would throw a ring into the sea to symbolize its marriage with the city, an event which is recreated in a short ceremony acted out by the mayor in the morning.

First Sun. after Ascension: Vogalonga, a marathon row around the city. This traditional non-competitive regatta departs from the front of the Doges' Palace for S Elena in Burano, and returns via the Canal di Cannaregio and the Grand Canal, covering 32 km.

June-Oct.: Biennale (see **A-Z**).

Third Sun. in July: Festa del Redentore, involving the construction of a floating bridge of boats stretching from Dorsoduro to the Redentore (see **CHURCHES 3**, **A-Z**), and a dramatic evening firework display, followed by a great deal of merry-making which continues through the night and traditionally ends with a morning dip off the Lido (see **A-Z**).

First Sun. in Sept.: Regata Storica, commemorating the legendary rescue of brides carried off by pirates during the Festa delle Marie, consists of a procession of boats and gondolas along the Grand Canal - a magnificent spectacle.

21 Nov.: Festa della Salute, commemorating the end of the plague of 1630 with a procession across two floating bridges over the Grand Canal to La Salute (see **CHURCHES 3**, **A-Z**).

Feltre: 30 km north west of Venice. Pop: 21,000. Train to Belluno and local bus. A remarkably picturesque town in the Dolomites. Many of its medieval and Renaissance houses are decorated with charming frescoes, the most noteworthy being those in the Via Mezzaterra and the Via L. Luzzo.

The main square, the magnificent Piazza Maggiore, is surrounded by superb Gothic buildings. At its centre stands a statue of the Lion of St Mark, a reminder that Feltre once was under the dominion of Venice. The Museo Civico at Via L. Luzzo 23 has an art gallery exhibiting Venetian and Italian paintings, and a small archaeological collection (1000-1200 Tues.-Fri., 1000-1200, 1600-1800 Sat., Sun.).

See **EXCURSION 1**.

Fondaco: A *fondaco* (from the Arab *fonduk*, meaning 'inn') was simultaneously a warehouse, a hostel for merchants and a diplomatic mission. The most notable remaining examples of these buildings are the Fondaco dei Turchi (see **GRAND CANAL 1**) and the Fondaco dei Tedeschi (see **GRAND CANAL 1**).

Food: Traditional Venetian dishes are often variations on other Italian dishes, with fish and seafood replacing meat (seafood risottos and grilled fish being great favourites). Specialities include:

risi e bisi - a thick rice and pea soup made with chicken stock.

pasta e fagioli - a pasta soup.

fegato alla veneziana - veal liver with onions.

polenta - a savoury food made from cornflour, which resembles porridge and is served with meat or fish.

bigoli in salsa - dark wholemeal spaghetti in anchovy sauce.

seppie in nero - squid cooked in its ink.

granseole - spider crabs.

moleche - small grilled crabs with soft edible shells.

baccalà alla Veneta - salt cod, Venetian style.

risotto ai frutti di mare - seafood risotto.

sardele in saor - sardines with onions.

Pasta and risotto are normally served as a starter, so make sure you leave room for the main course!

Frari: The Franciscan church of Santa Maria Gloriosa dei Frari is one of the finest examples of Gothic architecture in the city. It was begun around 1330, but took over a century to complete. The interior is surprisingly uncluttered (reflecting the taste of its owners), although there are several first-rate works of art, including Titian's *Assumption* (which inspired Wagner to write the *Meistersingers*), Giovanni Bellini's superb triptych of the *Madonna and Child With Saints* and sculptures by Sansovino (in the Corner chapel) and Donatello. The church also contains Titian's tomb (designed by Zandomeneghi), as well as those of a number of doges, and the extraordinary pyramid which encloses Canova's heart. See **CHURCHES 2**.

Galleria Franchetti: A marvellous collection of art works housed in the Ca' d'Oro (see **GRAND CANAL 1, A-Z**), which was assembled by its last owner Baron Giorgio Franchetti. Exhibits range from bronze statues and medals, to frescoes and paintings by artists such as Bellini, Mantegna (the well-known *St Sebastian*), Signorelli (the tiny *Flagellation*), Guardi and Van Dyck. See **MUSEUMS 2**.

Gesuati: The order of the *Poveri Gesuati* was absorbed into the Dominican order in 1668. Their church, also known as S Maria del Rosario, was completed in the mid-18thC and is the work of the architect Giorgio Massari. Exquisite ceiling frescoes by G. B. Tiepolo adorn the interior, which also features notable altarpieces by Ricci, Piazzetta and Tintoretto. See **CHURCHES 3, WALK 1**.

Gesuiti: The *Gesuiti* (Jesuits) were expelled from the city in 1606 and only readmitted into Venetian territory half a century later. Their ostentatious church (also known as S Maria Assunta), built in the early 18thC, reflects the great wealth of their patrons who included the Manin family. The overwhelming green and white marble-encrusted interior may represent the height of bad taste or the pinnacle of Baroque art, depending on your own taste. Whatever you decide, make sure you see Titian's fine *Martyrdom of St Luke*. See CHURCHES 2.

Ghetto: Despite the fact that the Republic had always been relatively tolerant of Jews, it was decided in 1516 that all Jewish residents should be confined to a small island in the Cannaregio district in the north of the city. This area was known as the ghetto because it featured a number of foundries (the Venetian verb *getar* means 'to cast metal'). As the number of Jews living in the Ghetto Nuovo increased, they were quickly allowed to settle in the neighbouring Ghetto Vecchio (the 'Old Ghetto', confusingly) and, later, the Ghetto Nuovissimo. Conditions remained cramped however, and the only way to alleviate the situation was to add extra storeys to the existing buildings. For this reason the houses in the Ghetto are the highest in the city.

Despite the restrictions on their movements, the Jews succeeded in establishing a self-contained and relatively prosperous community. Indeed, when restrictions on the movement of Jews were lifted by Napoleon in 1797, many chose to remain in the Ghetto. Even today, there are around 1000 Jewish people living here. The area has a unique atmosphere and features many traditional Jewish shops, synagogues and a small museum (see MUSEUMS 2). See WALK 3.

Giorgione (1476/78-1510): Giorgione da Castelfranco died of the plague at the age of 33. Little is known about his life, his training or even his paintings. Despite this lack of information, we know that Giorgione's influence was enormous, especially on Titian and Piombo. *The Tempest* (see **Accademia**) and the Castelfranco Altarpiece are among his most famous works.

Giudecca: See CITY DISTRICTS.

Gondola: The gondola is the oldest and most characteristic means of transport in the city and dates back to the 11thC. Until the 16thC wealthy Venetians took great pride in the appearance of their gondolas, painting them in bright colours and adorning them with elaborate decorations. By 1562, however, rivalry between nobles over their gondolas had become so intense that it was decreed that all gondolas should be painted black and bear no trace of decoration whatsoever. The basic design of the gondola remained the same until the late 19thC, when Domenico Tramontin developed an asymmetrical design which compensated for the fact that the gondola was propelled from one side only, and so enabled it to travel in a straight line. Few gondolas are now kept for private purposes. A trip down the Grand Canal in a gondola is still an unforgettable and romantic experience, if rather an expensive one. See **Transport**.

Gothic: A style of European architecture prevalent in the 12th-16thC, characterized by narrow pillars, pointed arches and high vaults. Gothic buildings in Venice include the Palazzo Ducale (see **DOGES' PALACE**,

A-Z), the Ca' d'Oro (see **GRAND CANAL 1**, **A-Z**) and the Frari (see **CHURCHES 2**, **A-Z**).

Guggenheim Collection: See **GRAND CANAL 2, MUSEUMS 3, Palazzo Venier dei Leoni**.

Hairdressers: These are distributed widely throughout the city and some of the more luxurious hotels have their own salons. The following hairdressers are recommended:
Lily's, Campo Guerra, S Marco 5364. Tel: 5222901.
Franco, Calle Larga, S Marco 658. Tel: 5238906 (superb, but expensive, women's stylist - L. 30,000-50,000).
Da Benito, S Marco 594. Tel: 5286221 (classy men's hairdresser).

Health: Before leaving the UK you should obtain form E 111 from the Department of Social Security, which entitles you to free medical treatment while you are in Italy. Present the form to any (State) doctor you consult, who will then arrange for you to be exempted from payment. Most dentists are private (fee approx. L. 60,000) and it often takes more than two months to get an appointment. Doctors and dentists in the city usually speak some English. Hospitals with an outpatients' department include:
Ospedali Civili Riuniti, Campo SS Giovanni e Paolo. Tel: 784516.
Ospedale Provinciale di Mestre Umberto I, Via Circonvallazione 50, Mestre. Tel: 981200.
Ospedale del Mare, Lungomare d'Annunzio 1, Lido. Tel: 5294111.
Ospedale Fatebenefratelli, Cannaregio 3458. Tel: 783111.
See **Emergency Numbers**.

Insurance: You should take out travel insurance covering you against theft and loss of property and money, as well as medical expenses, for the duration of your stay. Your travel agent should be able to recommend a suitable policy. See **Crime and Theft, Driving, Health**.

Laundries: Launderettes are scarce in Italy, and there are few in Venice. The most central is Lavaget at Cannaregio 1269 near Ponte delle Guglie, where you can do your washing yourself (tokens available from the attendant) or have a service wash.

Lido: A long, narrow island bounding the eastern edge of the lagoon, which shields the city from the effects of the tide. It was developed as a bathing resort in the 19thC and became one of the most fashionable holiday destinations in Europe. Though the glamour of those days has faded, traces of it remain in the grand hotels along the *lungomare* (seafront), most notable of which is the Hotel des Bains, the setting for the book and film *Death in Venice*. There are also other, much older, sights worth seeing. The mid-16thC Forte di Sant'Andrea, a masterpiece of military architecture which is, unfortunately, gradually being eroded by the sea, stands at the north-eastern tip of the island. Also in the north of the island are the church and monastery of San Nicolò, originally founded in the 11thC but reconstructed in the 17thC. The Lido is also the centre of sporting activity in the lagoon (see **Sports**), the location of the summer casino (see **NIGHTLIFE**) and the venue of the annual film festival (see **Mostra del Cinema**).

Longhena, Baldassare (1598-1682): One of the most important Italian architects of the 17thC. He was born in Venice and his most significant works are to be found here. The most famous is, without doubt, the church of La Salute (see **CHURCHES 3**), a masterpiece of Baroque architecture. Other notable works by him include the Ca' Pesaro (see **GRAND CANAL 1**, **A-Z**) and the Ca' Rezzonico (see **GRAND CANAL 2**, **A-Z**), his last work which was not completed until long after his death.

Lost Property Offices:
ACTV (Public Transport System), Corte dell'Albero 3880. Tel: 780310.
Stazione Santa Lucia (Railway Station). Tel: 716122.
Municipio (Town Hall), Ca' Farsetti (see **GRAND CANAL 2**), San Marco. Tel: 788225.
Poste Centrali (Main Post Office), Fondaco dei Tedeschi (see **GRAND CANAL 1**). Tel: 5220606.
Questura Ufficio Stranieri (Police Station - foreign visitors' department), Castello 5053. Tel: 5203222.

Madonna dell'Orto: An elegant church founded in the 14thC, rebuilt in the mid-15thC and extensively restored in recent years. It is said that a local clergyman found a miraculous image of the Virgin in a neighbouring garden (*orto*) and later decided that a church should be built there in honour of this extraordinary discovery. One of the most impressive Gothic buildings in the city, this was Tintoretto's parish church and many of his works decorate the splendid interior. It houses other notable works by Giovanni Bellini and Cima da Conegliano. See **CHURCHES 2, WALK 3**.

Markets: Venice flourished as a mercantile centre with strong trading links to the East throughout the period of the Republic. Exotic goods poured into the city and were unloaded at the markets beside the Rialto on the Grand Canal. Today these markets are as lively as ever. The two main ones are the Erberia, a fruit and vegetable market which also sells souvenirs and clothing; and the Pescheria, the fish market.
Markets in other areas of the city include one in the Campo S Maria Formosa (morning only, food and clothes) and another on the Rio Terrà

S Leonardo in Cannaregio. Both are usually bustling with commercial activity and you may find some good bargains.

Mestre: A mainland industrial and commercial centre at the entrance to the Venetian lagoon. Mestre and the industrial zone of Marghera constitute the modern, aesthetically displeasing, side of Venice. However, there are a number of good hotels and restaurants in these areas.

Miracoli: Situated in east Cannaregio, Santa Maria dei Miracoli is a remarkable Renaissance church built by Pietro Lombardo in the 15thC. The splendid exterior is clad in subtly-coloured marble, and the interior contains superb, ornately-carved choir stalls and small sculptures by Pietro's son Tullio. See **CHURCHES 2**.

Money: Foreign currency and traveller's cheques can be changed in banks and bureaux de change on the production of a passport. There are two bureaux de change (*cambio*) at the station which are open 0800-1900, but these often have long queues and the commission is higher here than elsewhere. Hotels may also exchange money for you, but again you may be charged a higher commission and given a lower exchange rate.
There is an American Express office (0800-1945 Mon.-Sat.; tel: 5200844) near the Campo San Moisè at S Marco 1471, with an automatic cash dispenser for American Express card holders.
Credit cards and Eurocheques are accepted by most of the larger shops, hotels and restaurants. Some establishments also accept traveller's cheques as payment, but expect to be given a lower exchange rate.
See **Currency, Opening Times.**

Mostra del Cinema: This international film festival takes place annually, at the beginning of September, in the Palazzo del Cinema on the Lido. Two weeks of all-day screenings of major international films attract well-known film-makers and numerous film stars. Tickets for screenings are usually hard to come by, but ask for information at the tourist office (see **Tourist Information**).

Murano: An island to the north of the city well known for its glass industry which dates back to the 13thC. The Museo dell'Arte Vetraria (Glass Museum) in the Palazzo Giustinian displays over 400 items of glassware dating from the 15thC (1000-1600 Mon., Tues., Thurs.-Sat., 0830-1230 Sun.). You can also go to the local glass factories and watch the glass-blowers and craftsmen at work.

No one should leave Murano without paying a visit to the wonderful 12thC Veneto-Byzantine church of Santa Maria Donato which has a magnificent mosaic floor. The church of San Pietro Martire, with magnificent altarpieces by Giovanni Bellini (see **A-Z**), stands nearby. See **LAGOON**.

Museo Correr: A magnificent collection of works of art and artefacts relating to the history of the city assembled by Teodoro Correr, a Venetian aristocrat, and donated to the community in 1830. The museum is divided into three sections:

First floor - Raccolte Storiche. Everyday objects and works of art from the period of the Republic.

Second floor - Pinacoteca. An impressive picture gallery displaying Venetian, German and Flemish paintings. One of the highlights of the collection is the *Two Courtesans* by Carpaccio (see **A-Z**), which Ruskin rated the best painting in the world.

Second floor - Museo del Risorgimento. A museum devoted to the history of Venice from the fall of the Republic in 1797 to World War II, with particular emphasis on the heroic struggle of the Venetians against the Austrian occupation of the mid-19thC. See **MUSEUMS 1**.

Museo del Settecento ('700) Veneziano: A superb museum in the Ca' Rezzonico which recreates the interior of an 18thC Venetian house and gives some idea of the splendour in which the wealthy inhabitants of the city lived in those days. Note in particular the grand staircase, at the top of which is an elegant ballroom containing carved furniture by Broustolon and marvellous trompe l'oeil paintings by Crosato. Among the other exhibits are superb frescoes by G. B. Tiepolo and paintings by Francesco Guardi and Pietro Longhi. The third floor houses a puppet theatre, an 18thC pharmacy and a collection of ceramics. See **MUSEUMS 3, Ca' Rezzonico**.

Museo Storico Navale: Appropriately situated beside the Arsenale (see **A-Z**), this museum consists of a fascinating collection of model gondolas and ships. A boat repair yard has been recreated on the third floor. See **MUSEUMS 1**.

Music: Classical concerts and operas are held regularly in the Teatro la Fenice (see **A-Z**) and the Teatro Malibran (see **Theatre**), and there is an annual Festival of Contemporary Music (Sept.-Oct.). Jazz features in one or two clubs, including Ai Postali on the Fondamenta Rio Marin and the Linea d'Ombra wine bar at Dorsoduro 19 near the church of La Salute. See **NIGHTLIFE**.

Newspapers: Foreign newspapers and magazines are sold at kiosks at the station and in many newsagents in the centre of town. *The Herald Tribune*, an international English-language newspaper sold throughout Europe, is widely available.

Nightlife: Venetians generally retire early, so there isn't a great deal of nightlife in the city. Eating out is the main social activity, followed by a pleasant stroll round the streets or a romantic trip along the canals in a gondola. For details of bars, clubs, restaurants, etc, see NIGHTLIFE, RESTAURANTS, **Music, Theatre** etc.

Riva degli Schiavoni

Opening Times: These vary from place to place and can change during the year, but generally:

Banks - 0845-1330, 1445-1545 Mon.-Fri.

Shops - 0900-1230, 1500-1930 Mon.-Sat. In summer, however, many shops choose to remain open at lunchtime and on Sundays. Under SHOPPING we have stated if a shop normally closes on any other day.

Post Offices - 0900-1900 Mon.-Sat.

Churches - 0800-1200, 1700 to dusk (subject to frequent changes, normally closed during services). Only opening times which differ from the above have been given in CHURCHES.

Museums - see MUSEUMS.

See **Public Holidays.**

Orientation: Note that house numbers do not refer to the number in the street, but to the number in the *sestiere* (see **A-Z**), making locations difficult to find using postal addresses (which only include the number and the *sestiere*). We therefore also give the street name in all cases. The following are some of the more common Venetian names for types of streets, squares, etc (alternative dialect spellings are indicated as these sometimes appear on street signs):

Calle - street; *Campo* - square; *Campiello* - small square; *Corte* - courtyard; *Fondamenta* - walkway along a canal; *Molo* - quay; *Ponte* - bridge; *Ramo* - short calle linking two streets; *Rio* - canal; *Rio te(r)rà* - filled-in canal; *Riva* - street along a quay; *Ruga* - thoroughfare; *Sali(z)zada* - the main street in a *sestiere*; *So(t)toportico/So(t)toportego* - narrow passageway or alley

The streets in Venice are labyrinthine in many areas and it is difficult for the first-time visitor to orientate him/herself. Buy a detailed street map with an index of street names. The main routes between the station (Ferrovia), Rialto and S Marco are clearly signposted (in yellow).

Padova: 41 km south west of Venice. Pop: 230,000. Trains every half hour from Venice (takes 30 min). A fine university town featuring outstanding works of art and architecture. The most noteworthy building is the church of San Antonio, known as il Santo, a stupendous 13thC Byzantine structure housing superb bronze sculptures by Donatello and the green marble tomb of St Anthony of Padova (in the Cappella di S Antonio). The tomb is decorated with intricate bas-reliefs by Sansovino (see **A-Z**) and Antonio and Tullio Lombardo, which are considered to be among the finest works of 16thC sculpture in all Italy. One of Donatello's most important sculptures stands outside the church: the imposing monument to Erasmo da Narni, known as il Gattamelata (a mercenary who became one of Venice's most successful military leaders). The Museo Civico in the Piazza del Santo boasts an impressive collection of 14th-18thC Venetian paintings (0900-1330 Tues.-Sat., 0900-1300 Sun.). However, the city's most important works of art are in the Cappella Scrovegni in the gardens of the Roman Arena. Here you can see one of the most influential series of frescoes in the history of western art, painted by Giotto between 1305 and 1310. See **EXCURSION 2**.

Pala d'Oro: This golden, jewel-encrusted altarpiece is the Basilica's most valuable treasure. It was begun in Constantinople in 976, and was commissioned by Doge Pietro Orseolo. Once it was brought to Venice, successive doges commissioned local artists and craftsmen to add further decoration, including precious stones and enamels  brought from the East by Venetian tradesmen. It is said that when Napoloeon's soldiers pillaged the Basilica they could not believe that so many precious stones and metals could be real - so they left the Pala d'Oro where it was! See **BASILICA DI S MARCO**.

Palazzo Ducale: The residence of the doge (see **A-Z**) and the seat of the Venetian government, at once a magnificent work of art and the symbol of the Republic's wealth and power. The first building was constructed here in the early 9thC, but the present building dates from a phase of radical reconstruction in the 14th-15thC. It consists of three wings constructed in a Gothic style, but clearly showing a Byzantine influence in several places. The main facade, on the south side overlooking the canal, is clad in a delicate pink Verona marble and white Istrian stone. The first floor has a superb loggia of intricately carved arches which runs the length of the building and the ground floor features an elegant portico. Note how the columns have gradually sunk down, while the level of the pavement has been raised to compensate for the rising water level.

Despite its rather top-heavy design, the building retains an appearance of lightness, especially when seen from the lagoon, from where it seems to float just above the surface of the water. Twice a day there is a tour of the palace's secret passages lasting about one hour, which you should book in advance (at the ticket office or tel: 5204287).

See **DOGES' PALACE.** For opening times see **PIAZZA SAN MARCO.**

Palazzo Grassi: A massive Neoclassical palace built by Giorgio Massari in the mid-18thC. It remained in the Grassi family until the last member of the family died in the 19thC. Bought by Fiat, and exquisitely restored, it is now the venue for major international exhibitions. See **GRAND CANAL 2.**

Palazzo Venier dei Leoni: Also known as the Palazzo Nonfinito because only one level of the palace was ever built. The Corner family (see **A-Z**), who lived opposite in the Ca' Grande, prevented any further building which would spoil their unimpeded view of the lagoon. Note the carved lions' heads on the facade, after which the building is named. The palace was bought by Peggy Guggenheim in 1949 and now houses her priceless collection of modern art. She is buried in the garden along with her beloved pet dogs. The collection includes works by Picasso, Duchamp, de Chirico, Magritte, Pollock and Rothko. See **GRAND CANAL 2, MUSEUMS 3, WALK 1.**

Palladio, Andrea (1508-80): Undoubtedly the most creative architect of his time, Palladio was born in Vicenza, a city which he subsequently, almost single-handedly, revamped (see **A-Z**). Outstanding examples of his work are to be found throughout the Veneto region. You can visit magnificent villas he built for wealthy landowners and members of the Venetian aristocracy around the Brenta Canal and further north near Vicenza. In Venice itself (where he settled in 1570), his most notable works are the Redentore (see **CHURCHES 3**, **A-Z**) and San Giorgio Maggiore (see **CHURCHES 3**, **A-Z**).

Parking: The five main car parks with direct transport links to the city are at:

San Giuliano, beside the Ponte della Libertà which connects Venice to the mainland.

Fusina, south of Ponte della Libertà on the mainland (can be reached from the Via Romea).

Piazzale Roma, straight on from the Ponte della Libertà - expensive multi-storey car parks.

Tronchetto, on the right after the Ponte della Libertà - a huge car park. See **Driving.**

Passports and Customs: A valid passport (or identity card for some EC visitors) is necessary, but no visa is required for stays of less than three months. There is no limit on the amount of money you can bring in or out of the country, but amounts over a million lire must be

Duty Paid Into:	Cigarettes	or	Cigars	or	Tobacco	Spirits	Wine
E.E.C.	300		75		400 g	1.5 l	5 l
U.K.	300		75		400 g	1.5 l	5 l

declared on the V 2 form you fill out on entry. Any valuable antiques or objets d'art must be accompanied by an authorization of purchase from the Fine Arts Department (usually arranged by the shop where you bought the article).

Piazza San Marco: Bounded on all sides by astonishing buildings, this is without doubt one of the most beautiful squares in the world. Significantly, it is the only square in Venice to be known as a *piazza*, the others being referred to as *campi*. The first important buildings to be constructed here were erected at the beginning of the 9thC, when the inhabitants of the lagoon decided make the area the base for their activities (in preference to the existing 'capital' of Malamocco on the Lido). The area which now constitutes the *piazza* was, until the 13thC, covered with grass and fruit trees, and had a canal running through it. The basic layout of the *piazza* has changed little in the past 500 years, and it remains the centre of all Venetian events and activities. See PIAZZA SAN MARCO.

Pietà: La Pietà was an orphanage for young girls, founded in the

14thC, that gained fame through its choir, which at one time was tutored by Vivaldi. The church of Santa Maria della Pietà on the Riva degli Schiavoni was founded in the 15thC, but rebuilt in the 18thC by Giorgio Massari. The classical interior features a magnificent ceiling fresco, *The Triumph of Faith* by G. B. Tiepolo.

Police: There are two types of police in the city: the Carabinieri (tel: 520477), a military police force in charge of more serious crimes, and the Polizia (tel: 5203232), who deal with general crime and administrative problems, including lost passports and the provision of reports of theft for insurance claims.
See **Crime and Theft**, **Emergency Numbers**.

Polo, Marco (1254-1324): One of the most famous of all Venetians, Marco Polo was born into a family of merchants and, at the age of only 17, set out with his father and uncle on a four-year journey to the court of Kublai Khan. He spent the next 20 years of his life travelling around the Far East, and eventually recorded his adventures in a book which came to be known as *Il Milione*. He is said to have lived in Cannaregio near S Giovanni Crisostomo (see **RESTAURANTS 3**).

Ponte dei Sospiri:

The Bridge of Sighs is one of the most frequently photographed sights in the city. It leads from the Prigioni della Paglia (prisons) to the Doges' Palace. There are two parallel passageways inside which prisoners crossed on their way to or from the Inquisitors. The name is said to derive from the prisoners' sighs, which were clearly audible as they passed over the bridge. The bridge can be entered from the Palazzo Ducale (see **DOGES' PALACE, A-Z**). See **WALK 2**.

Ponte di Rialto: A bridge of Istrian stone built by Antonio da Ponte at the end of the 16thC and, until the construction of the Ponte dell'Accademia, the only permanent bridge across the Grand Canal. Da Ponte's design was chosen over others submitted by Michelangelo, Palladio (see **A-Z**) and Sansovino (see **A-Z**). There are a number of shops and stalls on the bridge itself.

Post Office: The head post office in the Fondaco dei Tedeschi, by the Rialto bridge (see **GRAND CANAL 1**), offers all the usual postal services, including poste restante facilities. The formalities for sending parcels abroad are complicated so ask at the post office for instructions on the different types of parcel and the way each should be wrapped. Stamps are sold at tobacconists (*tabaccherie*) and in some hotels as well as in post offices. The current rate for a postcard to any EC country is L. 550 (L. 750 to the USA), while a letter under 20 g costs L. 650. Letter boxes are red. See **Opening Times, Telephones and Telegrams**.

Public Holidays: 1 Jan. (New Year); Easter Monday; 25 April (Liberation Day); 1 May (Labour Day); 15 Aug. (Assumption); 1 Nov. (All Saints' Day); 21 Nov. (Festa della Salute - see **Events**); 8 Dec. (Immaculate Conception); 25 Dec.; 26 Dec. (St Stephen's Day).

Raccolta Peggy Guggenheim: See **GRAND CANAL 2, MUSEUMS 3, WALK 1, Palazzo Venier dei Leoni**.

Railways: Santa Lucia station has direct links to most major Italian cities and European destinations. Services are generally efficient. The fastest trains are the Trans Europe Express (TEE) and the Intercity (IC) which stop at major destinations only (reserve in advance). The Rapido (R) and Espresso (ES) are also express services and only stop at large towns. The Diretto (D), Locale (L), Accelerato (A) and Littorina (L) are all fairly slow local services which stop frequently. Enquire at the station about train times, student and OAP reductions, etc.

Redentore: Built in thanksgiving for the ending of the plague of 1576 (*Redentore* means 'Redeemer'), this church is one of Palladio's (see

A-Z) masterpieces. The cool, bright interior has an air of great serenity. Note the two important paintings in the sacristy: Veronese's *Baptism of Christ* and a *Madonna* by Antonio Vivarini. The church is the site of the annual Festa del Redentore (see **Events**). See **CHURCHES 3**.

Religious Services: Non-Catholic services:

Anglican church - St George's, Campo S Vio, Dorsoduro 870. Tel: 5200571. (0830, 1130 Sun.; matins: 1030.)

Jewish synagogue - Campo del Ghetto Vecchio, Cannaregio. Tel: 715012. (0930 Sat.)

Lutheran Evangelical Church - Campo SS Apostoli, Cannaregio. Tel: 5242040.

Evangelical Waldensian and Methodist Church - Campo S Maria Formosa, Castello 5170. Tel: 5227549. (1000 Sun.)

Greek Orthodox Church - Ponte dei Greci, Castello 3412. Tel: 5225446. (1000, 1200 Sun.)

There are Catholic Masses throughout Sunday in most of the city's churches. The 0900 Mass at S Giorgio Maggiore (see **CHURCHES 3**, **A-Z**) is conducted in Gregorian chant.

Restaurants: Most of the city's restaurants are concentrated in the San Marco district, although there are also many establishments in out-

lying areas such as Dorsoduro.

A trattoria is a small restaurant serving traditional Italian dishes, a good place for a light lunch as you need only eat one course. Pizzerias and *paninoteche* are good places for snacks, and Venice now has a number of self-service and fast-food outlets.

A service charge of around 15% is normally added to the bill and there is sometimes also a cover charge. See **RESTAURANTS, Food.**

Salute: The domed church of Santa Maria della Salute is one of the city's most impressive sights. Construction began in 1631, and the building was dedicated to the Virgin as an expression of gratitude on the part of the survivors of the great plague of 1630 (*salute* means 'health'). Longhena (see **A-Z**) spent the last 30 years of his life working on the church, but died before it was completed in 1687. The sober interior contains outstanding paintings by Titian as well as Tintoretto's *Marriage at Cana*. The church is the site of the annual Festa della Salute (see **Events**). See **CHURCHES 3.**

San Giorgio Maggiore: An island situated at the east end of the Giudecca (see **CITY DISTRICTS**), directly opposite the Piazza San Marco. The first church was built here in the 8thC and a monastery was founded beside it in the 10thC. Subsequently rebuilt in the 13th and 15thC, the monastery now houses the Fondazione Giorgio Cini, an important cultural centre. The present church of San Giorgio Maggiore was based on a majestic design by Palladio (see **A-Z**), but was not completed until 1610, long after the architect's death. The bright, spacious interior is typically Palladian. Among the many works of art contained within are two of Tintoretto's finest paintings, *The Last Supper* and *Shower of Manna* (1592-94), and (above the altar) an elegant group sculpture of the *Evangelists* by Girolamo da Campagna. It is well worth climbing the campanile for the breathtaking views from the top. See **CHURCHES 3.**

San Marco: See CITY DISTRICTS, BASILICA DI SAN MARCO, PIAZZA SAN MARCO, **Basilica di San Marco, Piazza San Marco**.

San Michele: Most of the island of San Michele is given over to a cemetery opened in the 19thC to deal with the problem of overcrowding in the main city burial grounds. The tombs of Stravinsky, Diaghilev, Baron Corvo and Ezra Pound are all to be found here. The exquisite little church of San Michele in Isola, designed by Codussi (see **A-Z**), was the first Renaissance-style church to be built in the city. See LAGOON.

San Polo: See CITY DISTRICTS.

San Rocco: The church of San Rocco was designed by Bartolomeo Bon (1489) for the members of the neighbouring Scuola Grande di S Rocco (see **A-Z**). The 18thC facade is decorated with sculptures by G. M. Morleiter. There are superb canvases by Tintoretto inside, including an *Annunciation* and some scenes from the *Life of St Roch*.

San Giorgio Maggiore

San Salvatore: A rather plain facade conceals a superbly original Renaissance interior which was designed by Spavento and completed by Sansovino (see **A-Z**). There are two works here by Titian - an *Annunciation* and the moving *Transfiguration*. San Salvatore also houses some important tombs, including those of St Theodore, the original patron saint of Venice, and Caterina Cornaro (see **A-Z**), the tragic Queen of Cyprus. See CHURCHES 1.

San Sebastiano: This 16thC church is architecturally unremarkable yet, of all the churches in Venice, it has one of the most magnificent interiors. The artist responsible was Veronese, who adopted it as his parish church from the time of his arrival in Venice until his death in 1588, during which period he worked tirelessly to decorate every surface of the church's interior with marvellous paintings and frescoes. See CHURCHES 3.

San Zaccaria: The remains of St John the Baptist's father, S Zaccaria, were presented to the Republic and buried in the first church of San Zaccaria (built in the 9thC). The exisiting building is an intriguing mixture of Gothic and Renaissance styles. It was begun by Antonio Gambello in 1458 and continued by Codussi (see **A-Z**). Giovanni Bellini's famous late masterpiece *Madonna and Child With Saints* hangs over the altar. See CHURCHES 1, WALK 2.

Sansovino, Jacopo (1486-1570): Architect and sculptor. A native of Florence, he came to Venice in 1527 and was made the Republic's official architect two years later. His most famous works are the Loggetta (see **Campanile di San Marco**), and, his masterpiece, the Libreria Vecchia (see PIAZZA S MARCO).

Santa Croce: See CITY DISTRICTS.

Santa Maria del Carmelo: See **Carmini**.

Santa Maria Formosa: The first church on this site was founded in the 7thC by the Bishop of Oderzo, who had seen a miraculous vision of a buxom (*formosa*) Virgin! The present church was built by Codussi (see **A-Z**) in the late 15thC. Note the grotesque carved mask at the base of the campanile. The harmonious interior contains Palma il Vecchio's masterpiece, *St Barbara*. See **CHURCHES 1**.

Santa Maria Gloriosa dei Frari: See Frari.

Santa Maria della Salute: See Salute.

Santi Giovanni e Paolo: San Zanipolo is the Venetian name for this huge red brick structure which rivals the Frari (see **CHURCHES 2, A-Z**) in its grandeur. Construction of the church began in the mid-13thC, but it was not completed until 1458. Inside are the tombs of no fewer than 25 doges and, curiously, one English earl, Sir Edward Windsor, who died in Venice in 1574. The marvellous Baroque altar is probably the work of Longhena (see **A-Z**). The church is packed with impressive works of art, but two particularly fine paintings (in the south transept) are *Sant'Antonino Giving Alms* by Lorenzo Lotto, and *Christ Bearing the Cross* by Antonino Vivarini. Giovanni Bellini's exquisite polyptych of *St Vincent Ferrer with St Christopher and St Sebastian* should also not be missed. See **CHURCHES 1**.

Santo Stefano: A beautiful 15thC Gothic church with an elaborate stone facade featuring a tall campanile which leans dramatically. Inside, note the ship's-keel ceiling and three works by Tintoretto: *The Last Supper, The Washing of the Feet* and *The Agony in the Garden*. Canova's monument to Giovanni Falier, his first patron, and the monument to Giacomo Surian by Pietro Lombardo and his sons figure among the church's more remarkable works of sculpture. See **CHURCHES 1**.

Scalzi: See **WALK 3**.

Scuola: The *scuole* (schools) were the meeting places of lay confraternities formed by groups of residents who shared some sort of common profession or origin. They worked together to provide mutual assistance, and carried out charitable works in the name of a patron saint. Prominent artists were employed to decorate many of the *scuole*, often with cycles of paintings depicting the lives of the patron saints. Thus today the *scuole* house some of the finest works of art in the city. See **MUSEUMS**, and below.

Scuola Grande di San Rocco: The most opulent of the city's *scuole* (see **Scuola**), founded in 1478. The building, with its sumptuous facade, was started in 1516 and finished in 1549 by Scarpagnino. The grand interior contains a priceless collection of 56 paintings executed by Tintoretto between 1564 and 1587. The most moving and spectacular of these is the *Crucifixion* (1565), in the Sala dell'Albergo on the first floor. There are also other paintings by Venetian artists, including Tiepolo, and some beautiful 17thC carved panelling by Francesco Pianta. See **MUSEUMS 2, San Rocco**.

Scuola di San Giorgio degli Schiavoni: Founded in 1451 by a group of merchants from Dalmatia (also known as Schiavonia), this *scuola* features an elegant facade which incorporates sculptures of *St George and the Dragon* and the *Virgin and Child With Saints*. It is better known, however, for the magnificent series of paintings by Carpaccio (see **A-Z**) which adorn the interior. These depict the lives of the patron saints of the Dalmatians: St George, St Jerome and St Tryphon, and constitute one of the most important pictorial cycles of the 16thC. See **MUSEUMS 1, WALK 2**.

Sestiere: In the 12thC the city was officially divided into six administrative districts known as *sestieri* - Cannaregio, Castello, Dorsoduro, S Croce, S Marco and S Polo. House numbers still refer to their district rather than their street. See **CITY DISTRICTS**.

Shopping: There is a wide variety of shops selling everything from haute couture and fine art to straw boaters and imitation Murano glass, but generally speaking Venice is not a cheap city. Make sure you shop around and compare prices and quality. The shops in S Marco tend to be the most expensive, for obvious reasons, so it's worth venturing further afield. See **SHOPPING, Best Buys, Opening Times**.

Sports: Lack of space dictates that few sports, other than rowing, take place in Venice itself. However, the Lido (see **A-Z**) does have many sporting amenities. Facilities available around the lagoon include:
Cycling - bicycle hire (on the Lido) at Giorgio Barbieri, Via Zara 5.
Rowing - contact the Società Canottieri Francesco Querini, Fondamenta Nuove, Cannaregio. Tel: 5222039 (June-Sept. 0700-2000 Tues.-Sun.; Oct.-May 0800-1200, 1300-1800 Tues.-Sat., 0800-1300 Sun.). The club is open to all, but you must be able to swim.
Sailing - boat and dinghy hire at the Excelsior Sailing Club, Lungomare Marconi 52, Lido. Tel: 5261845.
Swimming - there are public beaches on the Lido, but the water is somewhat polluted. Alternatively, there are (expensive) swimming pools open to the public at the Hotel Excelsior and the Hotel des Bains on the Lido, and at the Hotel Cipriani on the Giudecca (see **CITY DISTRICTS**). There is another pool at the Sporting Club Venezia in Via Parri.
Tennis - Lido Tennis Club, Via S Gallo (tel: 5260954); Tennis Union Club, Via Fausta, Lido (tel: 968134); Sporting Club Venezia, Via Parri (tel: 770722).

St Mark's: See BASILICA DI SAN MARCO, PIAZZA SAN MARCO, **Basilica di San Marco, Piazza San Marco**.

Teatro la Fenice: Campo S Fantin, S Marco. One of the most sumptuous theatres in Europe. *Fenice* means 'phoenix', and the theatre did indeed rise from the ashes after the original building was destroyed by fire in 1836. The interior is decorated in gilt and velvet, and can accommodate an audience of 1500. The theatre is open to the public outside rehearsal times, but usually closed in August. See **Music**.

Telephones and Telegrams: There are public telephones on many streets, in the station, and in bars and newsagents (displaying the blue and yellow sign). Older coin-operated phones take L. 100 and 200 coins, but some only accept tokens (*gettoni*) which can be purchased in bars, hotels, newsagents, tobacconists and post offices. Newer coin-operated phones take L. 100, 200 and 500 coins. Other phones operate on phone cards worth L. 1000 and 5000, which can be bought at tobacconists. It is best to make international or long-distance calls at the Azienda Statale Servizi Telefonici (ASST) department in the main post office (where you pay for the number of units used at the end of the call), or at a SIP centre. To direct dial abroad, dial 00 followed by code for the country (UK - 44 , USA - 1), then remember to omit the first zero of the city code before dialling the number.
Directory Enquiries - tel: 12.
European Operator - tel: 15.
Intercontinental Operator - tel: 170. See **Emergency Numbers.**
There is a 24-hr telegram service at the head post office (see **Post Office**), or you can send one by phone (tel: 186). A cheaper, more efficient alternative is the night letter/telegram which is guaranteed to arrive the following morning.

Theatre: See **What's On.**

Tiepolo, Giambattista (1696-1770): Probably the greatest Italian painter of the 18thC, this brilliant and versatile artist excelled at fresco painting. Among his most important works are the frescoes in the Palazzo Labia (see **WALK 3**), the Gesuati (see **CHURCHES 3**, **A-Z**) and the Scuola Grande dei Carmini (see **MUSEUMS 3**, **Carmini**). His son Giandomenico was also a notable painter.

Time Difference: 1 hr later than GMT.

Tintoretto (1518-1594): Jacopo Robusti's nickname derives from the word *tintore*, meaning 'dyer', which was his father's trade. His numerous, sometimes enormous, canvases were executed at remarkable speed. His best works can be seen in the Scuola di S Rocco (see MUSEUMS 2, **A-Z**), the church of Madonna dell'Orto (see CHURCHES 2, **A-Z**) and the Palazzo Ducale (see DOGES' PALACE, **A-Z**).

Tipping: Although restaurant and café bills usually include a service charge, it is customary to leave a 10% tip. Hairdressers, taxi drivers, theatre and cinema ushers, toilet attendants and guides also expect to be tipped. Porters should be given L. 1000 per item of luggage.

Titian (1480/85-1576): Tiziano Vecellio studied under the Bellini brothers (see **A-Z**) and worked closely with Giorgione (see **A-Z**) who influenced him greatly. For almost 60 years Titian remained pre-eminent among Venetian painters, during which time his fame spread throughout Europe. He worked at various European courts and was eventually made official painter of the Venetian Republic. His work can be seen in the Accademia (see **A-Z**) and the Frari (see CHURCHES 2, **A-Z**).

Toilets: Public toilets are scarce, but you will find some in the station and at the *albergo diurno* (a day hotel with showers, washing facilities and a left-luggage department) behind Piazza San Marco. There are usually also toilets in bars and restaurants, but be warned - standards of hygiene are not generally high.

Torcello: An island in the northern part of the lagoon, which was first inhabited by refugees from the mainland in the 5thC. The island gradually increased in population (to around 20,000) and importance, to the point where it rivalled Venice itself. By the 14thC, however, its population had been drastically reduced by an epidemic of malaria. Today only 100 or so people live on the island, but it attracts many visitors who principally come to see the magnificent Veneto-Byzantine cathedral of Santa Maria Assunta which was founded in the 7thC and partially rebuilt in the 11thC (summer 1000-1230, 1400-1900; winter 1000-1230, 1400-1730; L. 1000). The interior features some superb mosaics, and a covered walkway connects it to the pretty church of Santa Fosca. Opposite the cathedral is the Museo dell'Estuario, housing important archaeological artefacts and fragments of churches (summer

1030-1230, 1400-1800; winter 1030-1230, 1400-1600; L. 2000). See **LAGOON**.

Torre dell'Orologio: Designed by Mauro Codussi (see **A-Z**) in 1496. The clock face shows the time, the phases of the moon and the position of the sun. There is a huge bell at the top of the tower, which is struck hourly by two bronze 'Moors'. You can climb the tower to witness this, but make sure you stand well back as the figures prepare to strike! During Ascension week and Epiphany, statues of the three wise men and an angel emerge every hour from side doors to encircle a golden Virgin. See **PIAZZA SAN MARCO**.

Tourist Information: The Ente Nazionale di Turismo (ENTE) offices will

help you with any queries and advise you on such matters as accommodation. They also provide free maps. Their offices are at:
Piazzale Roma, tel: 5227402.
Stazione Santa Lucia, tel: 715016 (see **Railways**).
Piazza S Marco 71/c, tel: 5226356.
For information on museums and churches, you can also contact the Venetian Museums and Monuments Association, Piazza S Marco 63, tel: 710155.

Traghetto: See **Transport**.

Transport: The best way to get around Venice is on foot, but if you are feeling lazy or are in a hurry, the following forms of public transport are available:
Vaporetto and *motoscafo* - the local equivalent of buses. Run by the ACTV, they are a cheap and reliable way of getting around. The fare is L. 1700 (all destinations). A 24-hr ticket (unlimited travel) costs L. 9000, a 72-hr ticket L. 17,000. These are available from kiosks at vaporetti stops. Throughout this book the vaporetto route and stop is given in the form 'Line 1, 4, Rialto'. See map on inside cover for routes.
Traghetto - a small boat which shuttles passengers across the Grand Canal from selected points.
Gondola - a pleasant and romantic way to travel, but rather expensive (approx. L. 60,000 for the first 30 min). Agree a price with the gondolier before you set off.
Water-taxi - luxurious but expensive (normally L. 85,000 for four people, but often open to negotiation). You can pick them up at the airport, the Rialto, S Marco, the station and the Lido.
See also **Burchiello, Buses, Railways**.

Treviso: 30 km north of Venice. Pop: 90,000. Trains hourly from Venice (takes 30 min). An important agricultural centre, formerly an independent city-state and, from 1389, part of the Venetian Republic. The town is surrounded by impressive 15th-16thC fortifications while the centre consists of picturesque medieval and Renaissance buildings. The 12thC Duomo (cathedral) houses some notable works of art, including paintings by Bordone and Pordenone. The superb 14thC Gothic church of San Nicolò, with its simple but majestic interior, stands in the south-west corner of the town. There is also a fascinating archaeological collection in the Museo Civico at Borgo Cavour 22 (0900-1200, 1400-1700 Tues.-Sat., 0900-1200 Sun.). See **EXCURSION 1**.

Vaporetto: See **Transport**.

Veronese (1528-1588): Paolo Caliari's works are characterized by a highly decorative style, rich colouring and dramatic visual effects. Veronese came to Venice from his native Verona in 1553 and lived near the church of San Sebastiano which contains some of his finest works (see **CHURCHES 3**). Other important works by Veronese can be seen in the Palazzo Ducale (see **DOGES' PALACE, A-Z**) and the Accademia (see **A-Z**).

Vicenza: 51 km west of Venice. Pop: 115,000. Trains hourly (takes 1 hr). A beautiful, prosperous town completely transformed by Palladio (see **A-Z**) after it had suffered extensive damage during the wars of 1509-17. Among the city's most important buildings, and one of Palladio's masterpieces, is the Basilica, which was created by building a second classical facade around the existing Gothic Palazzo della Ragione (summer 0700-1200, 1430-1900; winter 0700-1200,1500-1800). However, the most unusual building in the city is the Teatro Olimpico, Palladio's last work (16 Mar.-15 Oct. 0930-1220, 1500-1730 Mon.-Sat, 0930-1220 Sun.; 16 Oct.-13 Mar. 0930-1220, 1400-1630 Mon.-Sat., 0930-1220 Sun.). The extraordinary trompe l'oeil stage was completed by Scamozzi in 1584. Opposite the Teatro is another fine work by Palladio, the Palazzo Chiericati, which houses the Museo Civico. It has fine ceiling frescoes and interesting 14th-18thC Venetian paintings. The elegant 13thC Dominican church of San Corona is also worth visiting, if only to see a late masterpiece by Giovanni Bellini, *The Baptism of Christ*, and a superb work by Veronese, *The Adoration of the Magi*.

Just south of the city centre, within walking distance along the Viale X Giugno, stands the magnificent Baroque Basilica di Monte Berico

(1688-1703), from where there is a magnificent view of the city and the surrounding countryside. Inside are paintings by Montagna and Veronese. Nearby, in the Via S Bastiano, you will find two splendid villas: the Villa Valmarana, housing sumptuous frescoes by G. B. and G. D. Tiepolo (May-Sept., am: 1000-1200 Thurs., Sat., Sun. & hol.; pm: 1500-1800 ; Mar.-Apr. 1430-1730 Tues.-Sun.; Oct.-Nov. 1400-1700 Tues.-Sun.; L. 4000.), and La Rotonda (1550-1606), designed by Palladio and considered to be perhaps the most successfully realized, and certainly the most influential, of this great architect's works (gardens: 1000-1200, 1500-1800 Tues.-Thurs., L. 2000; interior: 1000-1200, 1500-1800 Wed., L. 5000).

Vittorio Veneto: 70 km north of Venice. Pop: 30,000. Trains every 2 hr from Venice (takes 1 hr 15 min). Formerly two towns - Ceneda to the south and the old fortified town of Serravalle to the north - joined by the elegant Viale della Vittoria in 1886. Ceneda is now a modern industrial centre, but it does feature the fascinating Museo della Battaglia, devoted to the battles which raged in this region during WW I (summer 1000-1200 Tues.-Thurs., Sat., Sun.; winter 1600-1800, 1500-1700 Tues.-Thurs., Sat., Sun.). Serravalle's streets are more picturesque - note in particular the Via Martiri della Libertà with its fine Renaissance palaces. It leads to the Loggia Serravallese, a particularly impressive Gothic building, built in 1462, which houses the Museo del Cenedese containing an important collection of sculpture, archaeological artefacts and Venetian paintings (0900-1200, 1400-1900 Mon., Wed.-Fri., 1115-1215, 1600-1800 Sat., Sun.).

See **EXCURSION 1**.

What's On: Ask your hotel for a copy of the monthly listings magazine *Un Ospite di Venezia*, which is published in Italian and English and distributed to hotels. Alternatively, buy a copy of *Marco Polo*, another English-language magazine which reviews films, plays

Palazzi Centanni, da Mula, Barbarigo

and exhibitions, and lists events. If all else fails, ask for information at one of the ENTE tourist offices (see **Tourist Information**).

Youth Hostels: The youth hostel is on the island of Giudecca (see CITY DISTRICTS) near the Zitelle vaporetto stop, and is only open to members of the International Youth Hostels Association. The hostel is in a superb position with wonderful views of the Doges' Palace. As a result, it is almost always full during the high season and queues form outside every day at 1500. The lucky ones will have to pay L. 13,000 per night, and be back in the hostel when the doors close at 2300. The hostel is closed 15 Dec.-1 Feb. See also **Accommodation**.

Zattere: Means 'floating pontoons' or 'landing stages'. In Venice it refers specifically to the landing stages along the Canale della Giudecca on the south side of Dorsoduro, a charming part of the city with marvellous views of the Giudecca (see CITY DISTRICTS).